THE HAR
SEVE

The Good Ideas Ruining Our Children

Considering dysfunction
in our primary schools

BY THE SAME AUTHOR

Poetry
Makers and Destroyers
Love's Troublesome Journey
The Sex Doctor
Scotland's Saint
Wrong Ticket Home
Surveying the Wreckage
Let's go ahead, then!
Epiphany in Azure: Columba on Iona
Likabehandlingsplan: Sweden Considered in Verse

Education Series
The Belt Room
Curriculum for Excellence
Queens of the Reich
Relentless: The Death March to Educational Excellence
The A–Z of Educational Nonsense: A True Guide
    for Parents and Teachers

Biography
William Wallace
Robert the Bruce
Janet: A Life in Verse

See other Big Ride titles at www.glenntelfer.me

See author blog at https://senecacaledonia.blogspot.com

THE HARMFUL SEVEN

Glenn Telfer

Certain that someone out there likes this stuff

Published By
Big Ride
6/3 Pinkhill Park
Edinburgh EH12 7FA
Scotland

LEGAL DISCLAIMER

A catalogue record for this book is available from the British Library.

ISBN: 978-1-909297-34-0

e-pub 978-1-909297-35-7

Cover design by Glenn Telfer

Design by Wordsense, Edinburgh; wordsense.co.uk

Printed by CPI Anthony Rowe Ltd, Wiltshire; www.cpibooks.co.uk

Contents

Foreword

The Enemy Forces Arrayed Against Our Children

As we hope to prepare our children for their best future, parents have always been concerned about the form and content of their education in school. Traditionally, most have adopted a policy of leaving well alone. This was because teachers themselves were generally accorded a respected status and could be trusted, and also the pedagogy and curriculum content at primary school level remained a simple thing, modest in its wider ambitions, and perhaps best described as traditional and practical.

Within the last generation, however, the increasing use of IT and the introduction of a social justice agenda has resulted in a paradigm shift affecting every aspect of teaching; likewise, the near total feminisation of the profession and the imposed presence of a foreign-origin replacement population brings new problems, but no obvious compensating benefit. These technological and societal trends have served to increasingly undermine the state education system and draw down upon it special scrutiny and criticism. Those charged with providing this education, particularly at primary level, have been subject to similar hostile attention, with their own education considered as certificated rather than learnéd, and their pedagogy, personal experience and habits often deficient for their task with those we love the best. It appears as if thought leaders have abandoned our entire education system simultaneously with it being converged and repurposed, and left it unable to set a true value on things. Indeed, the levels of waste and stupidity is such that one may whimsically believe that the system is run by teenagers; however, although real, the silliness masks a wisdom whose real intent is as evil as it is ancient. We may laugh, but really, it's not funny!

With respect to the quality and value of the education, much of this concern, both fair and unfair, has been hyperbolically expressed by idiot parents and our fake news media, and thus needs no repeating; so I leave this windmill to some other Don Quixote. But some concerns have largely avoided justified scrutiny and it is to this group that I direct my attention.

In this volume, then, I wish to focus on just one aspect of this concern, and that is the use of primary schools as a first base in creating a radical mindset among our children under the guise of social justice and the good global citizen. The success of this project has depended on a number of preconditions being met simultaneously; a pre-indoctrinated cohort of teachers and administrators, lack of knowledge by parents of what exactly is being taught, parents denied any realistic input into their children's education while malcontents enjoy deference, and the relentless, generations-long campaign waged by activists and their various allies to promote this political activist agenda, while simultaneously shaming and silencing any who question it as ignorant, or as we increasingly see, even bigots.

Many questions spin off from even a little thought about this situation; who is behind this agenda, what is their intent, who legitimises the activist advice-mongers and feeds them from the public purse, what does the end point look like? And the most crucial question, what are the consequences for our children of being the subjects of such directed political activism? Do they become little soldiers for the various causes and help achieve, as apparently assumed, a fairer future society, like a big happy multicultural café, or, by going against the reality of things, something dysfunctional and dangerous? In addressing these questions we must start this exploration by dispensing with virtue signalling and manufactured outrage. We accept, too, that the road to hell is paved with good intentions.

And seven? In numerology seven is the most magic of numbers. Sensing a fearful concinnity between events unfolding in our schools and End of Days eschatology, seven deceitful powers seemed to suggest themselves for examination, as if representing the seven blasts of the trumpet in the Book of Revelations, which signals the apocalypse. Seven also perhaps to better evoke the power of the seven virtues, both as a counter force and as a talisman for our argument to speed it safely to your good conscience. There seems to me a sort of truth in this view of seven, although for reasons beyond my ken. And, lightening the tone, referencing more contemporary popular culture; The Secret Seven finding out just what's going on and The Magnificent Seven coming to our rescue. Alas, if only they were real!

Moral cowardice, criminally negligent and straight-up treasonous are value descriptions that could be justifiably applied to the caretakers of our state education; however, I believe the judgement should go beyond this. And so, I use the word evil in this work in describing certain developments, and by this usage I mean plainly what is commonly understood by it; a pre-meditated and fully self-aware intent to bring down on the unsuspecting and undeserving victim, their ruination. This is strong medicine to be spooning in school, but I have come to believe that the evidence allows no other interpretation. The evil we reference is a subtle, patient creature far removed from beating puppies or robbing pensioners; it can wear a nice face and appeal to the better angels of our nature. And its gratification travels a long road.

I approach this task occupying four qualifying categories: teacher, parent, man and old. The first two speak for themselves, the latter two deserve a brief word of explanation. Man, because the primary school is a feminised institution, women providing around 95% of the staff and by the necessary form of this, the interests, sensibility and working practices natural to themselves; but with the consequences of this being largely invisible to them. Although not to me. Old, because having started school in 1961, I have knowledge of other working systems. These being pre-IT, pre-PC, pre-child centred, pre-parental interference, pre-blame culture, pre-multicultural, and yet successfully functional. Indeed, I trow, the practical knowledge and habits acquired from my first teacher, Mrs McKay of blessed memory, achieved only by chalk-powered technology and a firm, though kindly, adult presence, to be superior to the now, measured by whatever metric one chooses. I have this as a reference for comparison, and I don't like what I see when I look at what is touted as improvements, and I like even less those doing the touting.

In this work I have deliberately excluded what is usually presented as empirical evidence; this is mainly due to disdain for the academic researchers and policy experts in this field and the typical zero worth of their studies. This allows us to better press ahead with the polemic and the reader, freed from such distracting garbage and disinfo, to consider the logic of the argument and the evidence of their own eyes. As noted elsewhere; not everything that counts can be counted, not everything that can be counted counts.

As I see and understand it, at a truly gigantic financial cost, our children's brains, instead of receiving coding for orderly habits and higher consciousness, are more like receivers for Trojans, tracking cookies, media garbage and deceitful memes. But financial cost is the least of our concerns; for much of the content of our, hubristically named, Curriculum for Excellence, lays the foundations for the further sabotage of our customs and institutions by these same pupils, while simultaneously wounding their minds – and all wounds kill eventually!

By the agency of traitor dupes, spiteful zealots, idiot bureaucrats and misguided teachers, this agenda is delivering moral and spiritual destruction to our children. And the damage starts in primary school.

It may seem that this claim is way too strong for the evidence, I wad that it were so. But it's not.

This is why I am here. Presumably, you too!

Glenn Telfer,

Edinburgh, March 2021

Key Concepts and Definitions

Key Concepts

Race guilt, precocious sexual awareness, grievance culture, pupil political activism, legitimisation of MSM news, box-tick solutions, virtue signalling, empowering delinquents, misdirecting girls, undermining boys, authority of UN, victimhood, pretend compliance, gender confusion, endorsing IT, poptrash distraction, worry about global problems, celebrate homosexuality, more screen time, praise for alien cultures, sponsorship of smart phones apps, use of PC language, transgender welcome, historical misinformation, responsibility for Third World issues, promoting disingenuous distinctions, false praise, false censure, mental health services, cultural shame. In short; the global citizen.

Approved Learning Outcomes

White self-hate, reporting a racist classmate to the authorities, exposing a homophobe via social media, charity initiatives for Africa and Asia, variable pronoun sensitivity, worship false gods, Victor/Victoria-sexual confusion and understand the proper use of condoms.

Some Definitions

Stupid male teachers means stupid male teachers.

Stupid female teachers is a misprint.

Rubbish parenting only refers to the male if a XX–XY partnership, or neither if both/all partners are all female or all male or all neither(then they become honorary XX parents). By definition, female single parents cannot be rubbish parents. (conditions apply – refer to manual)

Us means us and them means them. Us being those who are not them, and them thusly being all the others.

Ethnic native (aka native White) means us in Britain who historically own European haplotypes, but sometimes it just refers to Scotland. However, it can also refer to other excellent Euro good Whites, like Baltic littorals and former Commies, assuming sober. Even Spanish and South Euros are generally included as passing. Basically, then, anyone peely-wally enough to pass as kilted at pistol range. You'll be able to work it out.

Any implied criticism of anyone, or thing, who is not a full-blooded White male probably implies the exact opposite, except when it doesn't. But the latter naturally endorses the former.

Apologies

Re: HR and Education Department staff, and especially Head of Service, for any disrespect implied when referring to them as nearly useless. Nearly useless? Such an implication does not even begin to convey the vasty scale of my feelings: *I have no words, my voice is in my sword*.

Legal Disclaimer

All the above is possibly not completely true, including this disclaimer. Maybe, possibly and perhaps.

SOFTENING

1
Tolerance

*O judgement! Thou art fled to brutish beasts,
and men have lost their reason.*

Introduction

Tolerance: A Disingenuous Virtue

In the Utopian dream of our wise politicians, under the rubric of
Our Values, we would build a Brave New Scotland. This project
would naturally start in primary schools. Following the attack led
by tolerance, the supporting battalions of diversity and inclusion,
equality and equity, human rights and self-esteem, justice and
empowerment would sweep the old ways from the classroom. And
then everybody would cheer! Apparently, as per MSM incantations,
we need tolerance to make us fit for the future.

There is an increasing sense, though, that as the tolerance has
increased, schools have become increasingly intolerable. And
that paradoxically it is the spectre of intolerance that haunts the
classrooms and corridors. Could it be that the reality is actually so
contrary to our hopes? As someone reared up in simpler times, P1
in 1961, well prior to our current Curriculum for Excellence, when
values were silently promulgated, except for tolerance which was not
tolerated,[1] I am thusly qualified to compare before and after. It is my
contention that the first part of the tolerance programme has been
successful and there certainly is more tolerance in our schools than
ever before. And if this is what we needed, then we are certainly we
are getting it good and hard. What exactly it is we are getting we will
explore in this chapter.

I have to note, at our setting out, that I burst with a curious national
pride when I think of the distinction Scottish education has achieved
under the righteous banner of *Our Values*; no small feat when
we consider that we are in competition with the self-immolating
superpower of tolerance, Sweden. And while it is true that the

Swedes will disappear up their own black hole[2] before us, when one considers the head start they had, we have made up a lot of ground to find ourselves within our own event horizon. It is a shame for us, although not for those invested in this agenda, that such excellence in irony must be purchased so dearly costed to our future native stock.

In considering *Our Values*, I have chosen to focus on the particular form of tolerance (i.e., big T, proper noun Tolerance[3]) that has enabled the situation we now find ourselves in. In this work I intend for this tolerance to stand as both proxy and leader, the Queen of Values, for the other values listed in the first paragraph. This is in order to simplify the argument regarding these values, and avoid becoming tied up in definitions and caveats. For one finds, in considering such values, that they are fungible,[4] and merge into and depend on each other; in a sense, they are all different expressions of the same viewpoint and intent. Tolerance, however, is both the battle cry and the keystone that bridges the other associated values which were formerly considered as debatable, if not dubious, propositions for our schools to contend with; to become – as now claimed – central to our children's future. These other values owe their presence in this discussion to this tolerance; without it, I would not have had to write this, nor you to read it!

Our wise forebears recognised that mistaken kindness, unskilfully applied was not a social or personal good. Were they wrong?

I have tried as best as I can to resist parodying *Our Values*. Admittedly they do so themselves, but still the temptation to assist is enormous and I have surrendered to the siren call, but hopefully not so much as to undermine my serious purpose. This is because, for all their comic absurdity and meaninglessness, they are a mighty existential threat without scruple. They don't need to bother with definitions and consistency, for their true intent is not to build upon logical foundations. We can laugh at this clown world, but must never forget the danger they intend to visit on us; the tolerance they preach is not for you or yours. Just to make a simple statement in this arena is to confront massive and hostile social forces.

And so, turning from the flimsy refuge of whimsy, we return to the serious issue at hand; what is the value of values?

What Is Tolerance?

Personified into your gender of choice, Tolerance wears a kindly face in school and is easy to get on with, so solicitous is it to your wants.[5] Check the company it keeps – best friends with diversity, justice, progress, equality and equity (assuming you can tell the difference!), self-esteem, respect, empathy, inclusion, alternative family values, pride (modern homo version) and soft fluffy cushions – all the nicest isms!. Tolerance wants you to 'live your dream' and 'just be yourself', and so is very understanding if this includes fragmentary focus in class, incomplete classwork, lost homework, carelessness with school property, and constant water bottle top-ups and follow-up toilet visits. Tolerance is very supportive of disruptive children and their families; it fully accepts, on the teacher's behalf, that insolence, disrespectful language and idiotic parent complaints are part of the challenge that make teaching fun. And, of course, Tolerance especially loves anything that connects children and sex; indeed, challenging traditional stereotypes by means of sex knowledge, tranny reading hour, free future-sex choice and kinky counterfeits as role models, is a top priority.

If you were seven and a bit naughty, Tolerance would be your best pal and you might wish it was tolerant all the time. The only thing Tolerance does not like is what was formerly called normal or decent standards, but is now labelled intolerance. Tolerance is very intolerant of intolerance.

As a personal value, calibrated to your life and exercised with wisdom, tolerance helps us overlook annoying foibles of others and ignore hostile trivia; this is the *quid pro quo* that keeps our society running smoothly. As a societal value, however, tolerance is an occasional fruit of deeply planted, but ruthlessly pruned, core values, not their foundation. Fed too much of the milk of human kindness it quickly morphs to its evil twin. And once ensconced, there is nothing to protect us from idiots, hustlers, troublemakers and perverts. Discord and anarchy, follow apace. The continuing proliferation of novel identities, dysfunctional lifestyles and degenerate activities that demand public acceptance and support are a consequence of such societal restraints having been eliminated. When everything is possible, you get everything that's possible, and then some! Our wise forebears recognised this in many common figures of speech regarding the need for vigilance around tolerance. In our collective amnesia we have forgotten this wisdom.

Formerly, then, tolerance was regarded as a dangerous value because of this potential for subversion, and was therefore only conceded under limited and specific circumstances. However, a multi-generational campaign across many fronts has encouraged the public to conflate this circumspection with intolerance and then portray intolerance as an exclusively negative force in society; mean-spirited, inflexible, oppressive, just as the term is now commonly used as a criticism. And worse, they then claim it as a particular feature of the great enemies of progressive thought everywhere; namely, men and traditional institutions. This cruel, unseasonable beast of a value, in this view, is then in need of chaining if we are to achieve the kindly, free-spirited, future world we are told we want. But all the while, this viewpoint failed to note the crucial protective role played by intolerance against the various malcontents noted above. And, not least, in maintaining school standards. Intolerance was, in fact, the tock to the tick of social interaction. It was indeed proof of our certainty in our own social convictions.

A functioning school cannot be founded on tolerance

As it is presented now in our schools, tolerance is a virtue consciously promulgated as such; the right to explore and action alternatives, to express your opinions freely, to make your own choices free from judgement or sanction, to be who you want to be, to dream big. Considered thusly, with no further reflection, it may indeed seem a social and personal good. Perhaps a little hippy-ish in the phrasing, but still seeming like the foundation of the good society. In this view, there are apparently no downsides to tolerance and it almost seems as if there's nothing more to discuss! Indeed, this is the *Our Values* in practice that make us, *Us*! And after all, who wants to have a reputation (author and possibly present reader excepted!) as intolerant, with all its planted implications of indifferent to injustice, opposed to equality, and in favour of division and exclusion?

In this view, tolerance is the chief virtue of all because our listed and lauded school values are, as we have noted, wholly dependent on it for their widespread acceptance. Indeed, in the absence of tolerance *Our Values* could scarcely show their sardonically smiling faces in school. And, as promoting these values is now claimed as the purpose of education in Scotland, so too must tolerance be forever kept in our minds as the great good. Each value promoted under the auspices of Tolerance paves the way for other 'values' further along the continuum on which public education is repurposed, which in turn further strengthens the tolerance mindset. The need to conform to this mindset, helped not a little bit by the law when necessary,[6] does the rest. Their opposites, under the rubric of intolerance, considered as all the bad isms and phobias; the great bad to be fought against. Worse, this intolerance is apparently everywhere in our schools. As it must be, given that intolerance itself is presented implicitly and explicitly as a particular feature of European societies, and even of the genetic heritage of native Europeans; phrased thusly to avoid implicating those intolerant others of non-Euro heritage and to keep the focus on native Whites. And especially men, packaged thusly to appeal better to feminists and kill two birds (cocks, obviously!) with the one stone.

These are the parasite worms of word and concept that infect our children. And which they must come to know and believe, if they are to inherit the future that is wanted for them, by those who want it. As mandated by our curriculum.[7]

> Whatever tolerance is, it will be evoked to shame
> and beat you into acceptance of a viewpoint
> you do not share.

Not Sure What Tolerance Actually Is; Ask an Expert

We have seen that it is the intention of our putative leaders that our children, like ourselves, should associate *Our Values* with social progress and moral goodness. And that this association is formed prior to them understanding the meaning and value of these values, to say nothing of actual intent and final destination. But we thinking adults are confused too, even when aware of the intention.

What do the various values actually mean?

In considering this issue as it relates to schools, we realise that our values and tolerance have become ideologies and not just occasionally used words; however, despite this significant development one finds that tolerance (and indeed all our values) are never actually defined by their advocates beyond the level of childish circularity. The sensible thing to do, then, in this situation, is to put some questions about this to an *Our Values* expert. For example; questions regarding the meaning of the terms, the nature of advocacy and of second order effects anticipated at some future date. However, this examination need not bore down to the deepest level of recursiveness, for this is simple philosophy and the simplest of questions, with eyes open and nonsense detectors on, is sufficiently powerful to reveal the beginning of the truth about *Our Values*. Further, it is incumbent on the proposer to be able to argue their case with evidences. We, the sceptical public, do not need to be the clever ones. We just need to listen carefully. It is not sophistry on our part to ask such questions and expect an honest answer.

For example, imagine the following put to an *Our Values* expert;

Why have values had to be made explicit and a goal of education? What deficiency does this actually address among us native ethnic Europeans, who are probably the world's most tolerant people?

Who is claiming this need and on what authority? Who means a named who, and who gave them this authority? Who are these people; after all, they have a name and account address for the siphoned-offed public funds – and their consultancy fees!

Who is the 'our' in *Our Values*? Specifically who; I know it's not me, and probably not you, dear reader.

What happens to those who are not part of 'our' group, nor want to be? Specifically, what will be done to accommodate those parents who do not wish their child to be part of this social experiment?

What is the end point of tolerance in schools? Describe this future place, and how and where the downhill snowball of ever-accumulating rights and tolerances is brought to a halt – or not?

What evidence is there for the various claims of social betterment that accompany *Our Values* and tolerance? Evidence meaning an independent and properly structured review; and not the statements and re-statements of advocates and beneficiaries. What makes this from attempt different all the other follies of Utopian thinking?

Counter the claim that tolerance and *Our Values*, promoted as they are, cause the problem that they seek to address; the self-fulfilling prophesy illustrated! Of course, a problem never fixed provides *raison d'être* for activists – and their funding!

Counter the counter-claim that people resent manipulation of their feelings and being blanket-condemned for attitudes which they do not hold and behaviours which they have not exhibited. And that, in resisting this injustice, they often come to embrace the very thing that they are exhorted to reject.

What does all this cost? We already know who pays! Cost also means lost opportunity and the ramifying impact of such focus on a child's mind and school life.

And in the dream I thought I heard the truth behind the spoken word.

Asking any of those questions of, say, the proselytising head teacher at your child's school, a propaganda workshop meister or education department expert is to break into their Utopian fever dream and, by risking exposing their hollowness and hypocrisy, receive in reply a large gagging spoonful of pablum[8] of the 'We make no apologies for our ongoing commitment to progressive values, etc., etc., blah blah blah…' variety. Delivered with a self-righteousness set at radioactive level.

In reality, however, whether teacher or parent, one hardly ever finds an opportunity to ask such questions to a person authorised or able to answer them. And although the incorporation of such values carries significant obligations for the whole school and at every level from drafting policy to class practice, all the changes come through proxies (actually, doxies), at workshops, conferences and by instruction from HQ.[9] None of these experts are able to answer the most basic questions as indicated above. I know from direct experience at introductory workshops and conferences that trainers responsible for introducing any aspect of the whole values panoply are unselfconsciously ignorant of the topic they are to champion, not understanding the need for evidence, nor having it anyway! Unvisited by thoughts of second order effects, they are also unable to defend any of the propositions except by repeating the promotional slogans: *The correct values for future world justice…the compassion needed to tackle global issues like slavery and climate change…skill building diverse positive attitudes to tomorrow's world today* and suchlike cant. Imagine the entire programme developed and presented by council HR 'consultant partners' for a flavour of the bombastic stupidity attending such presentations. Here we find the ultimate expression of useless people, all on top dollar public salaries.[10]

It seems as if no one directly involved has thought about what they are doing at all – and this is because they haven't! And they haven't for two reasons; one, they lack the intelligence; that is to say, the thinking (for want of a better word) is at bureaucratic, HR department level. Two; most are converted to the causes that Tolerance fronts and therefore feel no need to critically reflect on their belief. Endless tolerance and imposed values seem like a good idea to them because it is what they wanted to do anyway! It has been opined that this focus on values, especially in its immunity to facts and to clearly seen contradictory evidences, has taken on many of the faith attributes formerly reserved for religions; or indeed, that it has become a secular religion, complete with its untouchable gods, high priests, blasphemy laws for the unfaithful, and with primary teachers as the temple prostitutes.

The tolerance advocate's interest, then, in promoting 'our values' is not philosophic, but strictly operational; in that, the true intent of such terms is to shame or otherwise prevent the listener from questioning, far less resisting, whatever the true goal that tolerance hopes to achieve. There is no need for advocates to know what such ideas actually mean, they just need to believe. And there is no need, following this opinion, for you to know it either, they just need you (as the listener, public, parent and pupil) to tacitly understand that when tolerance is evoked you must accept. Unwittingly revealed in this situation is the personal attraction of such advocate types to the coercive power they enjoy by default of embracing a philosophy that includes moral and legal sanctions – at last, the free-ranging tyrant they always were, finally unchained! It all boils down to a power game where the 'victim' forces you to engage with their particular fictional version of reality. In your interaction with them you lend credence to their gaslighting of you.

What you would find in your pursuit of what our values actually are, whether your queries were general or specific, is that no one would, or could, answer them. And to return to our original point, there is no possibility of determining by enquiry and evidence from advocates whether our values and tolerance is a good thing or not. Instead, in contrast, you would find that you are expected to accept the various social pieties and Utopian dream propositions that accompany these values without demur. You would also find that your questioning would attract the hostile attention of various low-grade witch-finders who, keen to demonstrate their virtue as per their MSM training, would openly attack the questioner as a bigot. This I have personally witnessed. This is a world of binary thinking, good and bad, white hats and black hats assigned accordingly. Tolerance, here, is the security thug with a big stick.

Appeals to logic or evidence have no relevance here; this new religion has no limiting principle on its claims, short of physical reality. Likewise it would do no good to indicate irony, far less hypocrisy, to the programmed fanatics who are the movement's mouthpieces. You would have no chance of scoring a hit. The age when uncovering a contradiction was damaging to an argument, or exposing hypocrisy caused shame, is long past. Fifty years of MSM has taught us that.

**Still not sure what tolerance is; that's the plan.
Ask an expert…don't bother!**

Let Us Consider Tolerance in Action

If we cannot find out the true meaning and intent of tolerance and its related values by questioning their advocates in the expectation of an honest and sensible answer, perhaps we can work out what it is by considering an example. Focusing on what it does in school we can work backwards, so to speak, and discern its operational intent freed from the definitions game and party boilerplate. For it was ever true in human affairs that actions speak louder than words and reveal the hidden heart.

Tolerance's favourite trope is inclusion. However, although this would make an excellent test case, it is too gigantic a topic for our purpose here. But let us not back out of the challenge and instead cut our cloth to its purpose by selecting inclusion's current favourite step-child as exemplar – the transgender pupil.

In this specific context, Inclusion has been described as; welcoming such children into the school community and being sensitive to their special interests. Stated as such this is eminently reasonable. This inclusion, bravely heralded by BBC *Newsround*, is arriving in force, post haste from the UN and EU. Indeed, the Scottish government has committed to the implementation of an LGBT-inclusive education package arriving 2021. And transgender toolkits have already been issued – don't worry, no snipping required in class yet![11]

As someone who traces their unhappiness to being wrongly sexed and wants to change this via surgery and lifetime commitments to drugs and therapy, the transgender issue is simple in itself and well-deserving of discrete sympathy, but also laden with unresolvable complexities and (literally) transforming implications; right away, discussions with children about this hardly seems a proper fit for the primary curriculum.

Indeed, it is a topic that should be viewed as an exclusive preserve of the involved child, their parents and mental health specialists; and exactly NOT that of the suddenly involved motley crew of activists, virtue signalling politicians, sex fetishists, miscellaneous malcontents, meddlesome teachers, tweeting hausfrau, random perverts and – finally, and not least – the prurient and confused interest of classmates.

The potential for discord is obvious and one would think that sensible head teachers and administrators would fight to keep schools clear of the danger in this, not least to themselves. For surely they view, in the near distance, the inevitable lawsuits attendant on the introduction? And later, following post-op regret, the school's tolerance and support being subsequently viewed as advocacy – and rightly so – by those post post-trans people whose lives have been ruined in the madness they embraced, and were putatively encouraged to by their school. This very situation has already happened in the USA. We note too that the potential of this process for garnering attention or reaping remuneration will act as a magnet to those seeking either. Or, both, with the inevitable involvement of the world's most dangerous parent, the Munchausen Mother; for here they really can have the sick child they always wanted. However, big T tolerance will not allow you to think this realism out loud in a school setting.

One would also think that the attention directed to trans inclusion precludes the discretion which would surely be the desire of those directly involved and that this approach would carry the silent support of other parents; who in actual fact need no lessons in tolerance.

Following up this point, we note that tolerance has enabled the issue of transgender inclusion to arrive fully armed, forcing sceptics to accept the concepts and precepts as if this is a settled topic in society, and its presence in schools likewise accepted as necessary, even desirable. Any opposition is therefore already contaminated by apparent intolerance of vulnerable and needful children. In this view, only bigots have queries. This last point highlighting the staggeringly obvious irony of the tolerance advocates (or more properly, mongers) that they create the very intolerance they claim to oppose by conflating scepticism with this programme with intolerance and bigotry. They don't mind creating this friction, indeed, it is oxygen to them with their false sense of moral authority – and intellectual superiority! In their world of binary thinking, everyone is defined by who they hate and what they oppose, not by objective truth. These issues connected to tolerance are not, then, matters of opinion or choice, but extreme moral signifiers. Thusly, in this view, one is either extremely good (them) or extremely bad (you). This moral component precludes a solution in rational debate: indeed, the radical mindset that they represent is rooted in the constant struggle to move past the current 'evil' onto the next 'evil'.

Considering further, we see that emotionally-laden attention has been poured onto this topic, creating a school drama involving victimhood, even martyrdom, but all the while creating a distinction which garners, from the child's viewpoint, adult attention. Such a situation could well capture the wrong sort of attention among some vulnerable, but otherwise non-transgender, children. The exact outcome from this process is impossible to predict; however, it is feasible to imagine a vulnerable and lonely child embracing trans as a sort of survival strategy, wherein such children feel protected by caring adults and at last relevant to themselves; perhaps as an alternative to other self-harming behaviours, like anorexia. At the other, less lethal end of the pathology spectrum, we could have children, for whatever reason, going through a phase where they become contrary; and, in trying to be different, perhaps even deliberately cultivating an eccentricity. Although worrying at the time they occur, such behaviours need not be a chronic problem and typically self-correct with time; however, in our current climate, such a child could unwittingly start a ride which may only end at a terrible terminus

Most of these outcomes here described are more properly located in secondary school. However, by this time, the child has already been deeply prepared in the worship of sexual pathology by the introduction to such ideas in primary school and relentless society-wide MSM exposure:

21 Celebrities That You Didn't Know Are Trans-Positive.

Celebrity Dads Who Are Gay or Bi.

The Future Family is Trans and Poly, Say Experts.

That such exposure risks fetishising a child's developing sexuality and can drive them, in their confusion, to alternative sexuality and destruction, is not regarded negatively by the sex-world advocates.

This situation is not without its effect on other children in school as they notice this attention, and perhaps minor celebrity, to their formerly fragile classmate; and become confused, perhaps resentful and even a bit jealous? This principle of children not understanding an issue as the adult wishes, but noticing the special attention, and orienting their will in order to capture some of this, of course applies to all the other aspects of our values. However, big T tolerance has silenced this concern, and the LGBT-Stasi enforce it!

You will note that no practical issues appear to have been addressed in trans inclusion. Such as how much department policy and written law can we expect to ensure this happens, and who frames and polices this? How are changes to be funded, how is this to be managed? How are problems to be resolved and by whom? Who pays for the lawsuits? Who carries the can? You will find that you are supposed to believe that good intentions will see everything through to that happy conclusion. To which consideration, you would wonder what is the end point of this inclusion?

No one involved in promoting this issue appears to have considered the implication of the normalising in a school setting of issues that otherwise connect with mental welfare, the management of which usually connects with out-of-school services. This is not a simple matter of addressing a need with pre-existing services, as such hardly exist. There is talk of providing such services in school, (Sexual Transition Adviser, Gaylife Mentor, Drop-in Sexual Identity Centre, etc.) and by this physical presence thus further normalising the issue. And further contributing to the stresses pending pupil angst, activist complaints and parent suspicions! We can be sure, though, that if such services were provided in school that this would be done poorly, obviously chronically underfunded (or claimed so) and be the subject of continual complaint and division.

Any concerns, spoken out loud, that you had about the suitability of the dangerously well-meaning, averagely young women teachers, or 'specially trained' mentors, to chaperone their increasingly confused charges across this far frontier of sex, would find themselves confronted by Tolerance wearing its angry face. It would remind you that: *Having attending an HR Transitions course, your primary teacher is fully trained to lead discussions and help your primary-age child to choose the gender/s that best fits their future life choices.* And too, lest you fail to understand that, in the new reality, your concern is 'not helpful to future progress'

Thusly silenced, you would then note in contrast to yourself that Tolerance is happy friendly with those who are the accepted advocates and, too, that those advocates remind your instincts of witches in their need for access to children, yet not having any of their own. You would intuitively know why this is and not even need to smell sulphur to become worried about the nature of the values that are being transmitted in *Our Values*.

Consideration of all these observations of tolerance and inclusion will reveal that this involves not the simple, well-intentioned helpmate we may have originally thought, but something with an agenda and a strong sense of the subversive. An agenda that is not at all weak and needful of support, as it would have you believe for the sake of leveraging guilt and sympathy, but introduced with powerful backers who will have their way against yours. One realises that tacit in the emphasis on tolerance and inclusion was the unbelievable notion, for you to accept, that our primary schools were actually places of bigotry and exclusion in need of tolerance and values. The fear of seeming intolerant leads one to not ask the questions about this that you want to ask. But allow me!

Then you realise that all along big T tolerance was a weapon against your integrity and a challenge to your courage. But why; what is going on?

End Effect

...and and then Tranni the trannysaurus used the power of self-belief to energise her newly implanted super V which saved everyone on the planet, except homophobes and racists. Afterwards, xhe and xher friends, Homboi and Lezzi, downloaded a safe GAYSEX educational video. (click the link for advice)

As with the actual end effect of inclusion best illustrating its actual intent, so too with all the other aspects of tolerance in action. Everywhere tolerance is evoked we can look to see what it actually does to better find what it really wants, knowing its claims are a lie to buy your compliance. And so;

What does tolerance want *for* our children?

What do the advocates of tolerance want *from* our children?

Something of the answer is immediately revealed in the intersection between Tolerance's various foci; sex, children, gender, free choice, grievance, race. Sex and grievance leap out as the keywords in this interest and, too, as eternal sources of societal discord, but now relocated from adult to child domains.

With the alleged massively increased need for child psychological services, super-stressed schools and the lawsuits massing on the horizon, the end effect of all this Tolerance and Inclusion is, ironically enough, not tolerance and inclusion![12] It does not seem, then, as if the long-heralded Scotland fit for the future will arrive by means of the Curriculum for Excellence anytime soon! However, those who champion for this future will stay optimistic, and not without reason when one considers the true power behind this revolution, that the fun-loving, foam-filled bathroom and shower stalls for all the genders (and ages) to share, will yet arrive – *Yaaay*! – and as harbinger of more celebrations to come. More *Yaaay!*

Meanwhile, within schools, the radical empowerment of sexuality, and the consequent obliged reference to it, incentivises sexual expression in primary-age children. Non-binary, queerness, transitioning, questioning, poly-and pan-, gender fluidity, etc., all enter the lexicon, along with oppression narratives and accusatory language; a rare example of an expanded vocabulary not being a good thing! It also plays havoc with their minds as they are not ready for such ideas, and especially so when formally introduced by adults. It is just not feasible to present such issues to children and expect them to understand this as a choice which they themselves may freely choose to make – or, rather, should make! Even should dissenting views be presented, they are not intellectually or emotionally equipped to choose between them. And, therefore, the party that operates the schools is in a position to propagandise its tenets and will naturally disparage those of other parties. 'Other parties' here, means you! As. has been noted with tragic irony; not old enough to pick their bedtime, but old enough to pick their sex!

It is not for nothing, then, that nature corrals such thoughts until maturity and hormones require them; ideas and practices introduced outwith nature's timescale can only bring confusion and misery. In this particular case, hyper-sexualisation, and the next step on this route, perversion; a world where children can boost their self-esteem by sexting, dick and fan shots, and doing pornos. This is why families traditionally protected their children from such, and perverts targeted orphans and father-less children. If Jeffrey Epstein was still alive he could have told you how this ends!

It is not a sufficient defence to claim that such topics are introduced sensitively by child sex experts or fully workshop-trained teachers; for, as we have indicated, such experts are nothing of the sort.

Indeed, they may be more accurately described as un-experts! Further, the desire to discuss such topics with children should by itself be a red flag, indicating the need for close scrutiny of such adults. Imagine, if ye dare, the nature of a private discussion between a 'questioning' (i.e., vulnerable) child and the future school's Sex Transition and Homo Plus Mentor. It would be reasonable to have concerns about the nature of such a mentor's fantasy world, and that this could compromise the neutrality of their involvement.

In addition, little allowance is made in presenting this material for the significant differences between boys and girls in respect of their developing maturity, natural level of interest, or the special inappropriateness of this topic likely being introduced to little boys by a young, female teacher.

This sexing of primary education is the psychological equivalent of the modern child's diet; overfed and malnourished at the same time! It presents an analogy equivalent to obesity – promiscuity.

This tampering with sexual polarity removes the one cast iron certainty that children held about themselves; that they were little girls or little boys, and instinctively understood their habits and interests and friendships in light of this fact. Thus, snatching in passing the innocent but self-bolstering beliefs that came with this; namely, boys are the best or girls are the best, respectively. Instead all the sex and gender talk in schools, reinforced like background radiation by BBC *Newsround* and TV and MSM everywhere else, serves to entangle them in contradictory obligations, perplex them with oppositions of interest and bully with forced pronoun usage.[13]

Moreover, this early sexualisation, before children have a developed concept of their own sexuality, is like a portal to a demonic world in which everything segues to sex, and, following this logic, to confusion, ennui or even sexual depravity. Children, having no understanding of adult machinations in this regard, could be led to an appalling terminus before they are out of their teens. Here, it is not just their mind, but their very soul that is corrupted: witness 'Amazing Desmond', the little boy pimped as a transgender advocate and paedo-fantasy icon – and 'celebrated' for this.[14]

> 2018 DESMOND IS AMAZING!
>
> 2020 CELEBRATING DESMOND. WOW!
>
> 2022 WORRIED ABOUT DESMOND. HE'S NOT LOOKING SO AMAZING NOW
>
> 2024 ANYBODY HEARD ABOUT DESMOND RECENTLY?
>
> 2026 DESMOND LAWSUITS TOP $1 BILLION
>
> 2028 POOR LITTLE GUY. RIP

Everything in this world view is about the sexual; the body, politics and grievance are all alike in being exclusively grounded in the sexual world. Boys and girls, like men and women, are inevitably seen as lesser versions of each other and in essential antipathy. All this stands in opposition to their spiritual development as complete beings in themselves and also, tragically, as future love partnerships. However, this view of a child as an essentially spiritual being, in need of being gently led to the transcendent, lest that open sacred space be filled with its hellish opposite, is one that, alas, finds no place in the sexed-up curriculum of tolerance and inclusion.

Predicated on personal discontent externalised and ever finding or manufacturing further complaint, tolerance and inclusion never finds a happy place; even a goal achieved brings unforeseen consequences or fresh resistance which seed further unhappiness.

It is in the nature of such a force that once it has done something, then it will do something else – this is an essential aspect of its transgressive nature. Enough is never enough. Once some former activity, preference or behaviour is included within the new norm, then some other transgressive power beckons big T tolerance to help it achieve its ambition. What think ye is next to take its place on the pride flotilla? Thus beginning its journey, supposedly to just acceptance, but eventually always to full persecution of those who do not clap with sufficient enthusiasm – perhaps like you. Whatever you may think of as Tolerance's next project, if ye dare, someone with an interest in sex and children will have thought beyond this. This has become an issue far beyond that of adult privacy and advocacy of human rights. And so our schools continually nurture social anarchy and plant the same in our children's minds. Could this end actually be what is desired, even unwittingly? Perhaps this partly explains the apparent pointlessness in the proliferation of new identities with their attached, militant taboos; in that these were not a response to some need or harm being done, but an expression of a deeper, malignant need. For we note that when an alleged intolerance is attacked, what in fact is claimed as intolerance is merely just the noticing of observable reality. In real life noticing the naked king does not bring the universal laughter of the story, but a flogging for the breach of protocol-and so too here. As noted, these forces brook no dissent.

Logically, there can be no end to this process; although in the real world all the inclusions will start to cancel each other out, and end the process in anarchy and the destruction of the institution in which it is operating. Viewed at its simplest, this process involves humans at war with their nature, which can only end in defeat. We create victims around identity and fragile children rush to embrace it, and in the ensuing chaos we lose respect for our traditions, laws and institutions – and ourselves.

Thanks to big T tolerance we make even more broken children for the more broken future. In front of our eyes our children are being turned into psychological weapons against themselves in a future requiring therapy and drugs to reclaim the psychological balance they were born with. We are becoming by this process, an utterly debased race with no higher culture and no sense of our own purpose beyond grievance. The godliness within us is to be denied and by this denial we lose our dignity and a reason to love ourselves; and in losing this, a reason to defend ourselves. We shall become fallen, and an alien people to everything we were.[15] This is Jeremiah's warning, and we're still not listening.

Here we have only been considering the childhood sexual revolution aspects of tolerance. However, as tolerance is the foundational justification for the entire social justice agenda, so then must this same power naturally express itself across the entire range of connected beliefs, activities and behaviour found in school. As each aspect of this set is legitimised, then by implication, so too is any other; thus illustrating the worst sort of synergistic effect. It is this irresistible presence of big T tolerance which underlies the apparent acceptance of – but certainly the surrender to – many of the dramatically dysfunctional behaviours exhibited by pupils, as well as the continuous low-level disruptions in class. We see, then, tolerance having a central role in an interlocking network of hostile intent, bad ideas and poor practice.

With but a little learning and wisdom it would have been apparent that, with tolerance and inclusion as ruling principles, the introduction of diversity and sexual identity politics into primary schools, with the express purpose of turning them into an engine for social change, must end badly? Many must have predicted this and then seen it happening, but yet found no voice or were allowed no platform anyway; why is this so?

It's almost as if it is as if we and our children are being used as pawns in a wider game. It's almost as if someone secretly hates us.

It's almost as if they want to destroy us.
Ah, now I get it!

Who Is Behind This?

Here we peel the onion:

Obviously, we see the programme-fronting activists and politicians and understand their role and motive. We realise that behind them are beneficiaries of various sorts whose real interests, whether sexual, psychological or pecuniary, while not admitted, are easy enough to understand in their own terms. None of these are the drivers of the 'our values' programme. Here we posit another layer, for whom the former are puppets. These are less easy to be described, for they usually are, as puppet-masters should be, invisible. They are also less safe to describe. They know themselves and this is sufficient for their purpose.

Looking forward to a future ideal of gay privilege and gender valence, it is understandable that sexual and gender liberation advocates would relish the chance to present their cause to children to create a new generation of believers. Thusly bypassing parental concern regarding the pornifying of culture[16] and more general hostile reference to dramatically increased morbidity and mortality rates from STDs,[17] psychological problems and drug use.

We would expect, along for this ride, so to speak, paedophiles and assorted lascivious experimenters desirous of the potential future bounty to themselves and their ilk. Likewise, those who argue for race or female advantage, positing this as an allied and necessary response to native White prejudice and patriarchal oppression respectively, would also want their place in the new curriculum. Indeed, the whole self-hating gang gathers together in the name of Tolerance to join in this kicking of social norms; our twittersphere termagants, activist lawyers, public purse pirates and miscellaneous child-less malcontents.[18, 19] But, as is always the case, these heralds of societal destruction are merely the public faces,[20] and not themselves the true force behind this. They are the zombie army that can be, and often are, immediately snuffed out when they forget who they work for, or are otherwise surplus to requirements.[21]

Over the years, these actors and beneficiaries of the progressive sexual and multicultural future have been viewed by the interested public as variously legitimate critics, self-aggrandisers or misguided accordingly. The societal costs they brought were generally regarded as an unfortunate bug within the system, rather than a conspiratorial intention. Those Jeremiahs and the occasional Cassandras who saw where this was going were, of course, ignored or mocked.[22] And especially if they noticed the particular tribal composition of the powerful 'cultural committees' that were able to drive things on. However, since the century's turn, the increasingly obvious role of the MSM (and particularly women's/teen magazines), advertising and i culture as committed allies of these groupings, has alerted some observers to some other purpose massing behind the 'good intentions' – and some other force behind it. Some parents wonder how it has come to pass that so many invisible employees of the UN and EU find themselves handsomely salaried for doing the apparently invaluable work of bending our minds to their will by the passing of charters outlining for us *their* values for *our* children.

Some teachers too (well, me and another guy) became aware of the increasing role of the so-called professional journals in carrying forward this propaganda in op eds of low to zero intellectual content, e.g., the GTCS magazine, *Teaching Scotland*, whose sole purpose now, properly viewed, is to do just this.

As with so much of the harmful seven agenda, until relatively recently, parents as a group had no separate awareness of these developments as they appeared to have no particular negative impact on their children's education. Or, in the case of some female parents, they were generally on-board with these developments, as both an inherent female commitment to 'being nice' and group virtue signalling. Perhaps too, the vestigial remains (surely, the last) of a professional regard and trust for the teacher soothed any developing concerns.

However, perhaps let loose too soon, the trans rights movement has, in the ongoing conversion of a dysmorphic mental illness into a civil rights issue, inadvertently revealed these usually hidden dark intentions to the wider parent public. They have noticed that not only are their children to be co-opted on behalf of the movement, but also possibly inducted into it due to the sexualised ministrations of the various chaperones for this confused new world. And not least, by idiot-dupe teachers.

Here the wicked power reveals its hand; for whatever else is going on, these unfortunate trans individuals are being used as pawns in a wider game whose initial intention is the chaos we see unfolding. Out of this storm will come a remodelling of our society, and especially its sexual parameters, to which the conversion of children to early sexualisation is central. The society which accepts trannyism proselytised to their children as a legitimate and practical expression of individual choice, is ready to accept anything. Following this, then, brainwashing them into infertility and porn addiction is, literally, child's play.

This has led many to reconsider the motives of the progressives behind this agenda: They are not honest cultural critics trying to incrementally improve things, but enemies trying to destroy our faith in our culture, hoping to tear it down in order to build a new version after the fashion of their own minds; a broken-families, multi-racial, multi-sexual bordello with them in charge. Ticking off the list in the mind as one notices it; children co-opted, teachers implicated, always funding for promotional literature and 'inclusion' courses, replacement of traditional stories and books, education bureaucrats 'just doing their job', politicians congratulating their own tolerance and 'principles'. A realisation that your quiet-life existence is increasingly based on daily tip-toeing around certain topics and hoping that your tightly self-monitored political correctness affords you some protection from the horde. Then, casting one's gaze wider; the new inclusive literature celebrated and genuine cultural glories lambasted, TV shows and adverts all feature the new approved versions of social life, radio-controlled teenagers fronting slogans, random shops and businesses manically proclaim the new global and sexual faith. And Hollywood, with their tribal, sex-trading owners and non-tribal sex-selling sluts, hurtling us into the abyss by ensuring that every portrayal of Western life shows us as irredeemably corrupt.

And then you see it all connects; a generations-long project to manufacture consent for a future world that is not ours. A plot focused inexorably on producing doom for us. This has not yet succeeded in its main mission, but has been successful in its secondary one of confusing children and silencing adult dissent. So that when T and I (i.e., tolerance and inclusion as proper nouns) arrives and pushes its demands, every source of societal power, such as a company boards of directors, college administrators, prominent politicians, senior bureaucrats and head teachers, all fold like a house of cards. Currently, it seems, no individual may stand on principle against this tide, and keep their job and reputation. Here, only group-think is acceptable.

In this situation one sees the scale of this attack; on the one hand, coming through our MSM culture to suck the spirit out of everything that defines and ennobles us, and filling the void with sexual and subversive images and propaganda, these altering our frame of reference so that any new abomination is just another notch on the fetish dial. On the other hand, inculcating children with the whole DIE (diversity, inclusion, equality) catechism and sexualising their world view before they have the knowledge to resist it. Here we recognise the satanic use of glamorous serpents, disguised as popworld celebrities, to whisper in our children's ears. The true assignment of these totally-controlled, advocate-whores is the promotion of sexual neuroticism and confusion, and the monetising of our children's future hopelessness and depression. And, for us parents, taking away from us that which is our purpose, the right to protect our children from hostile manipulating others and sexual exploitation. Thusly, we become lesser than we should be. Our broken spirit further saps our strength, and TV will finish the job.[23]

One could argue that every society has its outcasts and haters who wish it ill as blame and compensation for their own various ills, and that these simply following their inchoate impulses, allied to the bureaucratic nature of our schools and sensation seeking media, have led us to the current situation. And so, no shadowy influencers are needed. What seems like a conspiracy is, in fact, just the 'spirit of the times'. There is truth in this view, in that the world often operates in this seemingly random and superficial fashion; however, considering this issue at a deeper level, one invariably finds that what we call the 'spirit of the times', is ultimately the spirit of the masters.

Think of the organisation behind this one ambition manifested in so many ways. Consider how the deeply understood knowledge of our innate goodness and our desire to be reasonable has been exploited. Consider this apocalyptic ambition for us planted in our children. Consider our collapsing birth rates and demographic replacement openly celebrated. Consider the tacit message of all our media: we own everything cultural that you love. And we are going to shift and alter your stories and your heroes, or violate them as we see fit, to mess with your mind. And you will watch helplessly while this happens, unable to do anything to save them because of the confusion and guilt we have planted in you and your children. Your leaders cannot help you because we own them too. And all this because we hate you!

It's not a conspiracy when it's out from its underground lair. Our soul is the prize, our demise is the goal. It's a global war. Scotland is just one outpost. And, alas, without the benefit we formerly enjoyed in the days of Calgacus, of being at the edge of the world.

These enemies are the ones who own the platforms that control your knowledge of the world, your entertainment options, your advert images, who finance directly the enemy organisations or direct state monies to them, who marginalise and demonise and erase your defenders via this control, the ones who try to own your mind; but above all, they are those who you cannot criticise. All higher order thinking leads to the same place and the same people, like a Scooby-Doo cartoon ending when the villain is unmasked. However, this unmasking is a task each reader must do for themselves, partly to protect the author from accusations of bigotry and conspiracy, but mainly to confirm the truth that these developments are not organic to us, and to free oneself from the fear of noticing the most powerful of taboos. Verily, I say unto you, this is a simple matter; follow the money backwards through the advocacy organisations and specially placed activist-journalists, and see what you notice. Just pick one topic, it's the same story for them all.

They are who they always are, them with their pocket Shabbos goy and golems.

The Virtue of Intolerance

Our native good nature has been exploited to advance an agenda that is proving catastrophic for our well-being, and we have been manipulated to consider perfectly rational concerns at the dysfunction attendant on tolerance and inclusion instead as a manifestation of *our* intolerance. The kindly table we naively thought we were hosting for the formerly excluded, turns out to be regarded by the putative beneficiaries as their rightful tribute and our guilt admitted. Our weak hand thus revealed begins a process of surrender following surrender, and the enemy (for such they are), ever advancing their rainbow battle flag into the terrain vacated to them, constantly stake out a new perimeter of radical demands. Within the systems that we currently have, there is no easy way to control the outsized influence of such fanatics. And in every case we are lowering hard fought standards that will not be won back in our time. The thinking mind revolts from the evident falsehoods, and this results in dissonance and denial colonising our minds, while the mad thrive – at last in their own arena!

This assault on the normative and the insistence on the relativity of values leaves us powerless to criticise this oppression. Our European default attitude of conceding some ground in an attempt to be, and to be seen to be, reasonable, ever willing to indulge just a little more, just one more time, results in no *quid pro quo*, for this tolerance claim is strictly strategic. Indeed, extending good faith towards the progressive agenda in this battle is just asking to be sucker punched. Nor will exposing the logical contradictions of their beliefs do them any significant damage. Their binary thinking only permits extreme options of right and wrong, indeed, it specifically rejects context and nuance. Any opinion which is not explicitly in favour of their view is to be destroyed. Such advocates, literally, have no sense of shame.

Tolerance advocates reject context and nuance, only goodthink is allowed.

But what to do in such a situation when facing an ascendant enemy? Firstly, we must maintain a presence in public space as a rallying point for those parents who do not wish their children to be part of this project. Hence, us here!

The real end of the game for them is our total surrender, where all categories of rational thought are abolished. Not only must you clap, you must believe. As O' Brien in Orwell's *1984* noted to Winston, who prophetically represents us: *The thought is all we care about, Winston.*

This thought, though, is now set to become the focus as Orwell meets Kafka in Scottish schools with the employment of equality monitors, thus ensuring *Our Values* have got bite to their bark. This ominous development of school commissars, celebrated with honeyed words of brotherhood, but backed by the law, alerts the functioning parent to the seriousness of their child's predicament in the T and I multicultural school of the near future.[24]

Some have suggested that this madness manifested under tolerance is, in fact, the plaintive scream for help of a crazed beast begging to be put out of its misery. There may be a truth to this; however, as there is no disinterested external oversight of our school dilemma, there is no brake to these developments. The madness follows its own logic, the mad and wicked cannot help themselves, nor want to. And so, our pity here would be misplaced and lose us valuable time in organising to oppose the horror unfolding before us.

Within school: frustrated entitlements stoked by the self-esteem movement and victim culture, the language of accusation becomes normalised; too early sexual empowerment releasing demons, ennui and depression which powers the child mental health crisis; the fear of lawsuits and Twitter mobs; and behind it all stands Tolerance. This power is not liberating children, who just want certainty and order, not sex choice at seven.[25]

Outwith school: parental dissatisfaction with the radical social agenda daily proselytised in the classroom; the censoring presence attendant at school meetings; increasing awareness of lost educational potential; their child's unhappiness. Tension vibrates the air. And as things get worse, the crazy get crazier, the accusations more righteous and the believers double down on their errors and wish harder for their delusions to be real. But when the belief chain finally ends, others will be scapegoated; these others are probably you, dear reader. This is the terminus of our tolerance nursed in our primary schools; this story multiplied a million times everywhere in the White world.

And, with the rapid sexualisation of children in the media and in primary education, what comes next we wonder? Logically, paedophilia is the next domino to fall and activists are already busy prepping public acceptance through well-established playbooks; have some medical experts proclaim it as a sexual orientation, then frame it as a human rights issue involving the child's choice of free expression of their chosen sexuality, next sympathetic characters in TV and movies, MSM/magazine articles mobilising fem-teens apparently opposing the patriarchy, resistance mocked as bigotry and finally, anti-discrimination laws kick in to protect practitioners of this new human right. By then, half of the public will cheer. This is arguably a generation away, but it will come unless we stop it.

And then, too late perhaps, when native stock is further replaced, the Test of Reality reveals the awesome destructive power of Tolerance approaching, finally unmasked, bearing our imminent demise, while the world looks like out-takes from *Bladerunner*. The 'Aha!' moment arrives; there and then, we will appreciate the virtue of intolerance. Not as some censorious, fun-hating maiden aunt, or the eponymous movie scene White bigots always hanging out in badlands biker bars to pick on a long-haired, inoffensive stranger in tight jeans who may be gay, but as a crucial means of maintaining the bar of high standards, and especially as a protection against those who would destroy us. None of these remarks deny past injustices, nor deny that society has to make adjustments, but reference the eternal problem of how far is too far.[26]

Too far is now, when debate is crushed and when children are the targets of the 'adjustment' by malcontents and perverts operating under the self-given authority of the UN and EU, and other alphabet 'justice' groups, themselves fronting for those hidden tribal oligarchs who have a strong penchant for European misanthropy.

As has happened countless times before, so again we will beg for the return of that most masculine of virtues – intolerance! Our society was predicated on it and our future will be.

Hopefully.

2
Anti-bully Initiatives

Oh, you've really got me scared. Not!

Introduction

Yet Another Lesson in Second-order Effects

It seems like a good idea; abolish bullying. Let a thousand flowers bloom and butterflies fill the playground in place of mean words and violence. As prophesised, the lion will lie down with the lamb, when the bully and victim resolve their issue with a respectful discussion of their feelings. According to experts, the problem of bullying was, all along, due to the absence of anti-bully initiatives. Luckily, they know how to fix this with public funds. But is life really so simple that adding the missing anti can provide a fairy tale solution to this perennial problem of school life?

Let us consider the unseen effects of trying to fix human nature.

Anti: a word for our times.

I don't like how this prefix to the compound word has become part of the infant's lexicon. Right at the start of their journey through school 'anti-' introduces them to the idea of badness and dysfunction, then it never stops talking about it. This worms its way into our children's minds, subliminally challenging their innate decency by positing its apparent absence as a collective failing on their part. And hence justifying the need for corrective initiatives, assembly harangues, videos, workshops and all the bin-bound paraphernalia that accompanies the 'anti-' world. The children understand this before they understand the language in which it is framed. This is where and how our children are first taught to question the goodness of their society and to hate themselves.

And so to our question: How do school anti-bully policies and programmes stop bullying; I mean specifically; what do they actually do? What specific powers of insight and persuasion do they access that have not been considered thousands of years before? Is there any evidence for the efficacy of such initiatives, and especially against cost?[1]

The Backdrop

In the one event, opposing principles in ugly balance; fear and humiliation, felt bone deep and irresistible power, joyfully transcendental. Usually, the bullying was a one act play with a short run, sometimes a season, occasionally a long run like *The Mousetrap*; which title describes how the victim of a seemingly endless run of persecution felt. As adults we understand the corrosive effect of the bully, both in the practical sense as the child also understands it, and in the spiritual sense as something broken and sharp they could carry to the future. As adults too we can also see how it damages on both sides, although it takes genuine effort to have sympathy for the perpetrator.

Perhaps you remember bullying as a life lesson, even though as a child you did not know or understand such an idea. More likely, though, it shades to grey over time as most things do. Eventually, one comes to a better understanding of such incidents, seeing them as part of growing up and normally holding no special power in your future life – an important point to keep in mind.

In olden times it used to be a simple thing to identify a bully by their works, and just as easy to fix them by a dose of their own medicine; as a pupil once wrote on the topic during Anti-bully Week:

One day these four ninja turtles saw a bully beating up a fat kid, so the ninja turtles kicked his ass.[2]

These days are gone, alas. Although not the bullying, which it is claimed has got worse, and in many more digital ways, since the olden days of straight thinking where bullies were concerned.

But how can this be; for we have more action plans, posters and anti-bully talking shops in place than ever before. This surprising anomaly was also registered by a head teacher following a tragic bullying case in her school; how could such a thing have happened only days after the Anti-bully Week finished, she mused. Her surprise was followed by a pledge to re-examine policies and to double restorative workshops, which must have been a great comfort to the victim's parents. This surprise, and the surprising lack of ironic awareness regarding her pledge, is at the heart of this chapter's contention; that second order and tertiary effects, added to the fundamental uselessness of the various anti-bully initiatives, result in a combined negative impact on the minds and spirits of our children, spooling out into the future. And that this effect far exceeds in corrosive power the original behaviours upon which it is predicated. It wouldn't be the first time a cure has exceeded the disease. Or even fed it!

Our argument here rests on the contention that bullying is not an endemic problem in our primary schools to the extent that we need programmes to tackle it? Of course, workshop meisters, grievance mongers and public purse pickers would contend it is, just as if their income depended on it! This argument holds even more true for the various special forms of bullying considered under the rubric of racism and assorted sex phobias; all these basically made-up problems create the problem they draw public dollar to fix. Fix meaning 'fix'.

We are not here trivialising the bully's power, nor the hurt of the victim, but rather trying to consider this issue logically. Of course, you wish that bullying didn't happen at all and as an adult you naturally wish to stop it, for truly there is nothing more dispiriting to witness than a child intentionally hurting another. But how to sort this problem in a fitting scale is the challenge for educators. Given that the old school solutions, typically presented as smack, threaten or otherwise humiliate, although in reality usually an eye-level injunction, are off the menu, we are left with a talking cure. And here it becomes tricky, because where rights and wrongs are concerned, people (whether child or adult) don't always allow for simple solutions. And this is especially the case with the most common form of bullying – verbal. Complicating things further, the perpetrator can also be a victim, or rather vice-versa as a better way of thinking of it; in that the victim may be at least complicit, or even (perish the thought) deserving. And so the simple,' Here's the cause and this is the solution', seldom has the desired outcome. And so to our argument:

There Is No Crisis of Pupil Bullying

Children are social creatures and naturally form dominance hierarchies. These hierarchies are not by themselves cruel or oppressive things for we need such structures to efficiently arrange our activities and, by finding our level, confirm who we are. Such hierarchies are subject to constant change, and especially so in school with its attendant comings and goings. In this change can come some friction, which is the basis of most so-called bullying, at least in primary schools. Except at the moment it occurs, such bullying is, properly viewed, almost a nothing. And is best treated as such; not dismissed by an overviewing adult, but not exaggerated either. If the disputants can sort it themselves, then so much the better – and usually they can. In this case, it is best to quickly pass over the issue and let them learn their own lesson about sorting their own problems. If, however, the situation needs a bit of adult wisdom, then keep it brief and simple, lest the children come to believe that the issue is bigger than they felt it to be; for children emotionally read and then reflect back the adult's take on something; if a teacher makes it a big thing, so will they. It is unfortunate that in the feminised environment of the primary school, with the default female love of drama and over-talking an issue, this is too often the case. In any case, as such occurrences are emotional in nature, discussions involving adult logic and principles of justice are often not understood by children. Even if they listen!

...makes them think about the hurt others suffer and engage with group share methods of processing their anger issues. (Anti-bully Action Pack)

Imagine an adult writing this – and believing it!

Sometimes (and it really does happen), a child would be unaware that their actions constituted bullying, and suspecting this to be the case, one could attend to the problem with some discrete and kindly words between you and them. I can think of many examples where such bullying situations have been expertly resolved by such minimal adult intervention, but this success has not in any way been connected to anti-bully programmes. The children involved then fixing their own problem, while perhaps together sent on a made-up mission somewhere in the school that would get them out of the class for five or ten minutes. With no need to mention it again, except to perhaps give the former disputants a reward for some jointly undertaken task, ideally unconnected to the dispute. It would be wrong to consider these most common of childhood situations – the misunderstanding, the teary response and the occasional meanness that accompanies social manoeuvring in a busy class – as proper bullying and requiring mandated programmes to combat. All that's needed is a bit of wisdom on the part of the adult. However, this wisdom, and the opportunity for this to develop freely, is taken from teachers by rigid school policy and by obligated programmes such as we are discussing. In the light of this, the teacher can somewhat end up like the fragile child, never able to properly process slights and setbacks.

There is, however, a real crisis of bullying in school; but it is of teachers by idiot parents, school management, council whip-bearing overseers, enemy MSM and sociopathic pupils.[3] And the bullying of the anti-bully initiatives.

Talking Up a Storm

The heading title illustrates a first problem with our anti-bullying approach; in that the creation of such programmes formalises what is typically a trivial event and then often bureaucratises the response. In conferring a definition and a legitimacy, and possibly a management involvement too, on an apparent bullying incident, it becomes more real in the mind of the child. And often, by this same agency, worse; perhaps much worse! Further, by directly encouraging children to consider their relationship to bullying events and how much of it applies to them, rather than encouraging them to let annoying trivia slip by, they become used to hearing and perhaps using the vocabulary of persecution, whether in pursuit or denial of a claim; thusly helping to normalise the same. We have seen the same phenomenon with tolerance, where children can become too well-versed in the oppression narratives and adept at shifting blame or maximising the drama.

An end result of this new-found vocabulary of persecution, added to an incessant and exaggerated attention given to bullying, is that a child's egocentric nature can be supercharged and they can too easily imagine themselves at the centre of an injustice; which, in this context, can worryingly become a desired distinction. Social rank then risks being replaced by victimhood rank – as has occurred in adult society. A little arms race can then occur in the scramble to the top of the victimhood pile. And some children (usually girls) easily talk up a storm featuring themselves at the centre of a fantastical bullying drama, when in actuality only their princess privilege was thwarted. No blame attaches to children over this development, for it is an inevitable consequence of the opportunities provided and a somewhat rational response, as they understand it. And probably most children, at some time or other, and to some extent, fall victim to this temptation.

The Happy-sad Meeting of Entitlement and Victimhood

Here the seed of thinking of life
in suchlike terms is planted
from which in nature passing
comes to flower as oversensitivity
and the quick persecutions
which the fragile righteous deliver
to those who disagree with them.
As Greta hectored: *How dare you!*

One might think that in this misunderstanding the ensuing discussion of what is and is not bullying would be just the situation the programmes are designed to tackle; being bullied is, for example, the following;

- A big boy stealing your play-piece, eating it and threatening the same until summer break.

- Someone secretly misplacing or damaging your property, e.g., breaking your pencils, etc.

- Two big boys in P6 always trip you up and laugh when you fall.

- A big girl tells everyone that your mum is a junkie and a skanky hoor.

- A kid keeps using a cruel nickname for you and constantly says that no one likes you.

etc., etc.[4]

But being denied, rejected, thwarted or ignored, or simply not getting your own way is not bullying. Feeling sad and connecting this feeling to an unwitting classmate, is not bullying: *Please don't confuse them, Boys and Girls.*

However, context is everything here. And, as I have probably inadvertently illustrated, this is not a simple or clear distinction to make; and by introducing all the necessary caveats and qualifications in discussing what is and is not bullying, children can be left confused about something that formerly was understood instinctively.

It is my contention, then, that primary-age children do not have the necessary emotional maturity and intellectual abstraction to properly understand and usefully apply anti-bully programme knowledge to potential bullying situations. Being egocentric by nature, they overplay their victim status, or feel righteous in persecution. And although the programmes are assumed to account for this developmental shortfall, they don't.

Any lesson a child may learn about bullying is dependent on it directly connecting to a current issue, swiftly mediated, and not some randomly introduced programme, like Anti-bully Week. This, and suchlike year-round exhortations to niceness, have the same impact on children as attending an HR workshop on combatting mansplaining at work would have on an adult.

Tackling the Bully
by Restorative Conversations

After creating an atmosphere replete with so-called bullying in which adult mediated intervention is proffered as a solution, then comes the kick in the teeth! As we too often find that when there is a genuine problem, the adults are powerless to help the victim, as the perpetrator can also play the victim game. Sometimes getting their revenge in early, as the rugby saying goes. And what we are left with is just a conversation circle; introducing the victim to the essential hollowness of adult justice initiatives and the perpetrator to the delights of gaming adults, which can be played with no consequence to themselves, even if they are exposed as deceivers. It's all just talk, although arguably a useful lesson in realpolitik to those children able to accept it! Representing the institution, and all future institutions in the child's adult life to come, the teacher demands and enforces the right to intervene and regulate disputes; while at the same time often unable to enforce fundamental laws that are intended to protect the victim. Here we have, then, a proper lesson of how the world actually is; too often all the state enforces is not the law, but its right to enforce the law.[5] Not one of the favoured groups? Then school, like the law, tells you to GTF!

Nothing better illustrates this wrong-headedness of anti-bully current practice than any anything involving the appellative 'restorative'.

This refers to the concept and practice of avoiding attributing blame in the resolution of any dispute. On the face of it, a reasonable sounding approach. The idea is that, after sharing feelings, each side comes to appreciate the position of the other, and following a (possibly figurative) big group hug, persecutor and persecuted leave as understanding friends. Issue sorted! Sometimes this works, of course, but usually it doesn't. And anyway always introduces a corrupting principle. For restorative conversations are in fact more concerned with minimising repercussions to the mediators, and recording a successful result for the incident book, than with justice. Both parties in dispute know *in advance* that only a compromise will be accepted as a conclusion; this in effect means the victim surrendering some of the legitimacy of their complaint and accepting something of the persecutor's viewpoint, regardless of how ridiculous this is. This approach provides an added benefit to the persecutor by seeming to ameliorate, or even partially justify, the actual bullying act and also their motivating impulse. For restorative is about recognising feelings, and the bully's feelings have to be considered too. Any child involved in this charade would easily understand the sophistry of the process even without the vocabulary to describe it. Thusly, the principle of justice is hobbled from the start.

Real lived life is, of course, a compromise, and one could claim that this restorative approach is therefore in line with such realism; however, although I have been arguing in favour of downplaying school frictions, sometimes they are real and blame is deserved. Apportioning this should be the adult's job, performed without fear or favour. In seeking to avoid apportioning blame, and thus stepping aside from the judgement, restorative practices betray principles and children. Blame and punishment are not necessarily bad things. And the perpetrator can (inasmuch as their free will allows) come to accept their error and by this process also come to genuine apology and contrition. But whether they do or nay, they at least realise that there are painful consequences of their transgression. The victim sees justice executed on their behalf and has their faith in their society's institutions and the existential goodness of life confirmed.

As, crucially, do other children who have not otherwise been directly involved. The moral relativism of restorative justice does the opposite because sometimes blame is deserved and therefore the judgement too. By such judgements do we adults demonstrate a conviction in our own standards, and by such do our children learn our ethical code. Or not, as the case may be!

I contend, then, that the moral relativism of restorative justice is another force that ultimately undermines our collective commitment to societal and personal inner peace. Once again, we see that the true consequences of do-gooding are do-badding. The gods laugh at us. As do the true bullies – and why should they not?

Any teacher who thought to introduce some plain-speaking realism into a restorative discussion[6] could easily find themselves accused of bullying by the bully's parents; and then find that any subsequent discussion involving themselves and HR at council HQ, was not very restorative at all! Manipulative and sociopathic children sense all this early on, understanding this lack of consequence to themselves and may go on to enjoy seeing impotent, apologetic adults dancing to their tune; it may seem incredible to claim, but just one or two such children can ruin the well-being of an entire school, turning it into a sociopath's playground. Being involved, or even just witnessing, such events would be character forming; in all the wrong ways, of course. But all this while explicitly denying the one avenue that would offer the genuine victim, genuine respite – the direct confrontation with a clearly transmitted willingness to fight. Or just going straight to it, as one's best instinct instructs!

Anti-bully Programmes
Don't Work Anyway

In being exposed to anti-bully programmes children naturally go along with the propaganda and confirm what they've been told, by regurgitating the same rhetoric they've just been fed. Later, reviewing the correctly completed, anti-bully worksheets and recalling the parroting of shibboleths, the unthinking teacher may view this as evidence of the programme's success. The box has been ticked, however; they would be mistaken about the success of such programmes.

Note here that our argument is concerned with the formal programmes and procedures that have been imposed upon the teacher. We accept that a sensible adult often can provide a useful service in helping to resolve childish disputes and should do so if instructed thusly by their wisdom. However, sometimes it doesn't solve the problem and here the security-seeker child has to face themselves with this hard reality, and find a way of standing up to the bully. But by themselves! Courage isn't something that appears in ordinary life, but it must be summoned by the bullied child if they are to enjoy its corrective and redemptive power. That this may cause pain is the point of the courage and the source of their redemption.[7] Most children could find this power within themselves, and especially so with some adult encouragement, however, such a real world approach runs counter to everything the anti-bully policies and practice represents. In this sense, then, the entire anti-bully programme creates a culture that prevents those children trapped at the bottom of the social hierarchy from finding their own solution to their persecution and thereby a better ranking for themselves.

Lest it be misunderstood, we are not necessarily advocating that a child should punch (or, if a girl, slap and hair pull) their way out of the corner, although we are not advocating that they shouldn't either; but rather, the courage we wish a bullied child to find is firstly spiritual, and by orders of magnitude greater than the physical courage, which is merely the back-up. Often, just the willingness to directly confront the bully, with the implied willingness to resort to violence should this be required, is sufficient to preclude that violence, while resolving the problem.

The anti-bully programmes, by contributing to our children's over-protected world, reduce the need for self-initiative and courage. By so doing we downsize the spirit of our children to their long term detriment. For that spirit having never been accessed as a child may become tragically atrophied in the adult. It is one thing to run to an adult for succour at seven, but at thirty-seven?

Our ancestors would have understood this as beyond obvious. But we moderns are so far fallen from common sense that, as the Bible reminds us, there is no more remembering of the wise than of the foolish!

In short, then, the first and obvious argument is that the programmes don't work for those who need it, and isn't needed for those with whom it would work.

When we entertain and action an idea that proves disappointing, in our private life we have the liberty to admit this and replace it. When a mistake is made within a bureaucratic institution like a school, we have typically already activated the interest and funding of some agency who cannot be let go, especially if the idea they now front contributes to the prevailing mindset of the future dysfunctional society of White confusion, guilt and failure, as the anti-bullying agenda does.

The system absorbs this zeitgeist and moves on with it, denying the errors and waste by doubling down on them. Ever blaming others and lack of funding for any failure, this is the school equivalent of the revolutionary's credo of shooting ever more people as a response to their programme's failure. Like bullies, they will not let us escape from their anti-bully playground.

Our children and their teachers find themselves trapped by this prevailing orthodoxy. It's almost as if the anti-bully agenda, has another agenda. It's almost as if what they really want is...

Beyond the Present

An idea lives beyond the present when it shapes future attitudes and behaviour. What then would be the likely future impact of the anti-bully initiatives? In that realm beyond words, where children sense the real message behind arguments, what do they come to understand? It is my contention that this is the value of victimhood, either as plaintiff or as resentful observer. They become versed in its vocabulary. And note the high value that adult females place on discussed feelings and resolutions based on this. Only later, will they come to realise that men process such differently.[8]

Instead of bullying being something that might have happened to you or which you have done (both, of course, usually being the case), it instead becomes something that is everywhere, and so always in mind, but as a negative and fearful presence. Robust children generally pay little heed to such, but the fragile child is further sensitised.

I am a victim is a shortcut to being noticed.

Our digital isolation has made us desperate to be noticed. This also applies to primary-age children, as much of their lived life now lacks, in the loss to digital parenting and TV screens, the complete human attention of former times. It is inevitable, then, that anti-bully initiatives in encouraging complaint would unwittingly provide some of this attention. Little girls are especially susceptible to this incentive, as they, like their adult version, enjoy complaining for the opportunity it affords to talk about themselves and get others (especially boys) into trouble. The anti-bully programmes thus provide an early and easy introduction to the attention and complaint culture, and with it, at least initially, the belief that someone cares about your problems. Being a victim nowadays not only garners attention, but can even be glorified; here, the suffering itself dignifies the holder. Significantly, this merit is passive, enjoyed independently of struggle or dignity in adversity. The potential for this false belief undermining the natural development of self-confidence and an independent outlook on life cannot be overstated. In addition, by invoking adult intercession, it impedes the development of the natural hierarchies by which children sort their own problems of group dynamics, while simultaneously strengthening the subversive alliance of victims, snowflakes, tell-tales, cry-babies and malcontents. The teacher who subscribes to this anti-bully rationale and the concomitant policies and practices, unwittingly undermines in her pupils the very qualities she believes she is encouraging. And thus we arrive at the victimhood culture.

Victimhood Culture

Victimhood culture develops when a society evolves to handle personal slights and general disappointments via third-party intervention, e.g., school authority, police, or social media. Formerly, such were handled directly, or ignored if trivial. What makes this culture dangerous is that it incentivises 'victims' to record and broadcast every conceivable slight against them, no matter how trivial or unintentional. This easily segues to, firstly, exaggerations, and then, outright falsifying; both of which require the application of guile, long noted as a corrosive power in a child.

A parallel ratting culture is also created where everyone with a mobile can be a spy or, by feigning friendship, a double agent, by recording some indiscretion or joking remark for future backstabbing. Thus we have created Big Brother and his feminist sibling, Tittle-tattle Little Sister, the tag team of the victimhood industry. These provide daily examples via MSM to our pupils (e.g., # Metoo, # Believe her, # Anothermalepig, # Hatespeech@cop. scot, etc.) of how to think of themselves as victims and righteous agents of justice; obviously, this appeals more to females.[9, 10] And it is under the auspices of this approval that some children are encouraged to have, as it were, a trial run of combining victimhood and ratting out. No teacher, however, could simply call this out for what it really was, as they have encouraged the same via anti-bully programmes. The potential for discord within school, and then as this circle spins into adult life, is surely obvious. And, of course, double-victim bonus points are automatically earned if one also holds a race card. Equally obvious, when we widen the circle out from the personal, are the socially corrosive effects of this mindset, as well as the public purse costs of the various victimhood advocacy organisations and law courts. All this potential for attention, redress and pay-out perpetuates the problem. This strong social presence, vigorously reported (pot stirred) by MSM, thusly justifies itself and strengthens the apparent need of the whole anti-bully system from school curricula and workshops to law court. Thus do we create a self-perpetuating circle of self-destruction.

Those children who come to enjoy, or otherwise require, victimhood can become reluctant to leave victim paradise, and as the victimhood *dish de jour* loses its flavour will swap it for another equally tasty, but more topical. For this age is truly the golden age of the victim. The heroes and heroines of former times; stoic, brave, creative, contemplative or sacrificing, have been replaced with something exclusively self-centred and in keeping with our modern manic entertainment requirements. This dramatic shift in public attitude to adversity is a fairly recent phenomenon, as formerly one wished to avoid being seen as a victim or a complainer; a mindset endorsed by the 'stiff upper lip' and the adage 'keep calm and carry on'. Considering this thought further, the child complainers and tittle-tattles of our time who have completely misunderstood the anti-bully message, would have been given short shrift in my schooldays. And odds on that Mr Reid would have belted them; rationalising their desire to be a victim by fully obliging them![11]

However, such children who take advantage of victimhood will enjoy only a tactical, and oh so temporary, attention boost. For life's results are cumulative and those who come to view their life through the prism of victimhood would tend to find it a self-fulfilling belief, each disappointment further self-disempowering and setting up the next one. This point of view can become locked in for life. Such heavy handed signalling of weakness to others cannot end well.

Those other children, the vast majority in school, who view victimhood from outside its comforting embrace have their sense of natural justice insulted in the same way as the adult's would be when they see the complainers appeased, system gamers rewarded and the diligent, quiet majority ignored; that is, ignored again. The chagrin of this silent, uncomplaining majority gradually translates, as they age to adulthood, to private cynicism and withdrawal from public life. This is one means whereby victimhood culture destroys social trust. Case by case is our collective belief in the merit of our institutions and procedures is damaged. Considered thusly, the anti-bully programmes are another aspect of the White People Are Pigs project. As it must be apparent that all forms of bullying in schools by non-Whites, whether adult or child, are widely accepted either by redefinition or more usually by ignoring. Justice is not blind, it's just not for you! And especially you, if White and male, or, as it is now termed, extra-plus privilege!

The micro-aggressions, safe space, triggering and apologies demanded for faux offences, all these features of a spoiled upbringing which first manifest themselves in the teenage years do not spring fully formed at that time as if from the head of Zeus, but have been modelled and primed in primary school. This fragile and entitled behaviour is the first and bitter fruit of the anti-bullying initiatives. It takes training to be outraged ten times before lunch.

Victimhood culture is self-sabotaging.

It is a truth, apparently unknown in educational settings, that directly pursuing a social goal results in its exact opposite. By undermining self-solutions and feeding victimhood culture, the anti-bully policies provide a classic example of such contrary effects.

This phenomenon can be illustrated further when a child goes beyond an attention-seeking complaint and ends up bullying others by harassing them over hurt feelings, the so-called cry-bully phenomenon. This behaviour mirrors the pathology exhibited when former underdogs turn master; the so-called victim's rule paradox.

Such bullying 'victims' will probably acquire attention by such a route, but victim sympathy is a currency quickly spent, and attempts to obtain more credit eventually backfire. Tragically, disappointment over the ever reducing level of sympathy obtained can lead the victim to double down on their victimhood and become a cry-baby. And no one likes a cry-baby!

Don't say things that make you sound weak.

In this case, other children can then respond to whining with real bullying. That the bullied child unwittingly can create the situation they complain about is not so perverse to fairness as it may seem; for what we have here is an innate evolutionary response to the presence within the group of a weak individual who compromises its cohesion by whining to obtain privileged treatment; naturally this is resented. Human nature thusly may seem contrary, but the nature part knows what it's doing, even when the human part doesn't. With the lightest of adult touches, quite unconnected to policy and procedure, one can help with a natural resetting of this social balance. The real message of this is that saying things that make you sound weak, makes you weak. And an enemy of your better self.

Victimhood culture is feminising.

By encouraging the female love of drama, and talking about self as victim or hero in said drama, anti-bully policies contribute towards feminising, and feministing, firstly schools, and then the nation.[12]

One way that it does this by legitimising a female response to social friction; this being reporting and discussing hurt feelings as the correct response to bullying, and one which properly engages the higher authority, in this case, the teacher. All our anti-bully procedures are based on this approach. The female teacher naturally attempts to place the bullying issue into a social context and understands it as a breakdown of communications, which just have to be re-established to fix the problem. Whereas, this seldom describes the situation from the male's viewpoint – whose understanding is much more physical. The female teacher, typically unable to understand this feature of male psychology, thus provides a (female) social solution to what is often a (male) physical problem. Unlike the male, she is trying to understand and resolve a situation from a viewpoint that does not countenance physical violence. That this response is essentially feminine would hardly ever be considered by female teachers in their response to a bullying incident, or accepted should it be suggested. There is thusly no recognition that males process social friction differently, and should be allowed to do so. It is not reluctance or a character fault that generally prevents males from seeking adult intercession or discussing their hurt feelings in a restorative conversation, but a psychological template that evolved over the aeons. This is what makes the male a male. And a little boy must be allowed to engage with this maleness without judgement or censure. Of course, they too may wish to discuss an incident, but generally not so much and, anyway, conducted differently. They don't wish to talk about how they feel, but be told what to do.

The feminising nature of the anti-bully message implicitly tells the girls that they are right in their essential attitude to bullying and of how they process it; and so by extension of this, legitimising the accusatory and stealth manoeuvring so natural to females, but so disruptive to social harmony. This same message implicitly tells the boys that they are wrong. It also tacitly suggests its inverse; the girls 'know' that the boys are basically wrong in how they handle bullying, and the boys that the girls are apparently right in how they do it. Considering little girls, this reinforces the gynocentric viewpoint of superiority that is progressively ruining many females. With respect to little boys, what this does is to encourage a feminising of the male response; which puts males at a social disadvantage and at war with their basic nature, which is also progressively ruining many males. None of this is said of course, nor need be understood as such by children; like us adults, they absorb the habits and assumptions of their age, even when they sense old blood telling them different.

Boys Not Considered Yet Again

In the desire to prevent bullying it has not been considered that what we do impacts differently on boys and girls. Of course, there is overlap, but there are some effects peculiar to boys which have chronic personal and societal consequences. Moreover, such effects are not only unconsidered by the femcentric school system, but perhaps even unimagined. Two things stand out for consideration here:

Firstly, victimhood culture short-circuits the natural development of dominance hierarchies among males; these being the means whereby they self-organise to cooperate and keep the peace. In contrast to females, boys need few rules for this process to work as it is innate to their sex.

Men and boys are nearly always able to organise themselves for a task and self-sort their problems. Officious feminising of this process creates the very situation it attempts to address.

However, a boy who plays by the rules of victimhood culture and solicits third party interventions on his behalf forfeits his natural place in the male dominance hierarchy, as well as undermines the organic legitimacy of such hierarchies. This will not, of course, immediately lead to social ruin, but it is another subtle factor in the war against nature which always comes with too high a price; in this case, a boy's sense of honour attendant upon earning one's natural place in the scheme of things. This is no small matter in the life of a male, particularly when it is developing. For honour is the prime motivator of male standards and drive, and of self-regard. It obliges self-solutions, although not discounting peer support, whereas victimhood culture is the opposite.

The second, and most obvious, of these effects is the absolute injunction in the anti-bully coda against physical violence. Here I am meaning the retaliatory punch or wrestle, also known as a schoolboy fight: This must never be vigorously agitated against, far less removed from a boy's armoury. A boy, like a man, must always have this potential in reserve, for this is a feature of his character upon which his own sense of worth, our society's stability, and his future family's security, is derived. It is this ability that prospective life partners, perhaps unknowingly, seek as a guarantee of his maleness; will he stand and protect when that moment comes? That this is a last resort need not be emphasised, all males understand this; and this is ultimately what keeps bullies in check. To remove this attribute, as anti-bully programmes are wont to do, is to make him harmless, and by so doing, unmanly. And, ironically, a target for bullies, as well as a coward to himself.

Being a man in 2020: Think warm thoughts.

This is not an argument for violence – except when it is! But violence works, and accepting this is accepting reality; those few individuals who find a too easy recourse to violence can only be stopped by the same. This is the default lesson that the bully teaches all of us, and it is a most valuable one, because many situations in life have the potential to be suddenly distilled to their threatening essence, with the questioned posed or implied: What will you do about it? Unless you have already faced this situation, you probably don't know. But if you have acquired some experience in facing that moment, you can probably prevent the situation worsening, or even arising in the first place.

And claiming this is not condoning male violence. Indeed, as we have noted, by coming to understand something about violence, a boy comes to wordlessly understand something about himself as a male, and the role of honour and courage and physicality in the making of himself as a man – and by this understanding, a gentleman. Finding his own place in the hierarchy is part of the growing up process that is best not overly interfered with. Considered properly, then, direct conflict between boys in response to a bullying situation is not necessarily socially disruptive or personally dysfunctional. In an odd and counter-intuitive sense, the bully provides a valuable service to a boy in this growing up; for bullies are always present throughout one's life and a male has to understand how to cope with this on his own, and after his own fashion, in that space between surrender and outright violence.

The bully unwittingly provides early training in how to cope (or how not to cope!) with the sliding scales of persecution. And in addition, they may provide the victim with a bespoke awareness of their perceived, if not actual, weaknesses, for them to consider for correction. This is an example of a life lesson that really should to be sorted out when you are young, because it is so much harder to do when you are older. The anti-bully safety net compromises this necessary development. For the socialisation of boys has some need for direct challenge, as they, unlike females, do not possess the intuitive ability to negotiate (and charmingly backstab) around frictional social situations, or solicit (invariably male!) aid in their predicament.

At best, then, the anti-bullying programmes may help boys be protected from school-time physical violence, but at a cost to those protected as noted above. Many teachers may consider this protection sufficient justification; however, as (probably) women, most do not understand that for boys a school fight can serve a positive purpose for both boys involved, but especially the bullied or otherwise lower ranked boy. Not only does such a fight have the most ancient of pedigrees, it is also still the most respected solution by boys themselves. And, it has long been noted, that a scrap between boys can resolve a situation in a more genuine way than could ever be obtained by teacher led discussions or other adult interventions. This is Mother Nature's anti-bully programme, and she knows what she's doing, having done it forever!

Understanding how this process works is a great power for a boy to acquire, for it places him correctly in the middle of the violence continuum; not a quick-fisted thug, nor a pussy-pawed target. The recourse to violence is not always the right thing for a boy to do, of course, but the instinct is always right, even when the action is wrong. And sometimes the correct advice should be:

If he does that again, punch him on the face. Would you like me to show you how?[13]

This is very powerful medicine against a bully.[14] When the bully says: *Yea, you and whose army?* And the bullied child, in an army of one, raises their fists. This is what gives a boy the belief to pull the sword from the stone when that moment arrives.[15] This is why girls will love him.

Evil Concinnity

That the anti-bully programmes show no awareness of potential negative consequences arising may be a surprise to the reader. However, on considering the source of such, and suchlike, programmes, the surprise should disappear as quickly as the hoovered up public funds that went into making them. For although nameless, the developers hail from the departments of educational psychology, arguably the top phonies in the world of science, but certainly the most useless. Alas, this same lack of wisdom is also displayed by advocates and teachers as the implementers, this too is not surprising.

One has to wonder, though, given the monkey-level crudeness of these programmes, how apparently no one considered the surely obvious potential for unintended consequences. How could this be so; is there really no one at a higher level of planning carrying some wisdom? This thought leads one further to consider just how such ideas gain traction in the first place. It is as if, at some meta level of operation, the intent is not just to employ simpletons and raid the public purse with yet another nice sounding, but useless add-on, but something nefarious. And that the real intent is the actual end effect we are witnessing; simultaneously hubristic, destabilising and disempowering. And this especially so for native White children, to the extra extent that this agenda connects to racist and sexist claims. For we already know, as our children too soon learn, that in wider society there are certain categories of people (probably you, dear reader) that it is completely acceptable to marginalise, bully and even destroy their livelihood. It seems as if we are training an entire generation of native White victims to accept verbal and physical bullying as somehow deserving and be morally disarmed against taking their own side, while they surrender their defence to some other authority. Presumably, this is because diversity and inclusion are so much more important than protection from bullying, false accusations and loss of societal trust! It is our tragedy that such protection will surely be needed; for studies show that people with a heightened sense of victimhood (real, perceived or fabricated) generally express, not a desire for reconciliation or to 'let it go', but an increased desire for revenge that simmers until the opportunity arises to action it. Doubly hobbling for native Whites is the evidence that such individuals and groups tend to see their use of aggression and violence as morally justified, while seeing the same by their opponents (which will be us) as unjustified and morally wrong. Alas, all this was completely predictable.

A final consideration is that where anti-bully initiatives have encouraged pity and neediness, they have encouraged revulsion to the same extent. This is especially the case with boys, who risk rejection by male peers and aversion by females. A boy cannot know this, but if he unwittingly incorporates, via anti-bully programmes, such a strategy of minimising threat and hurt, he will in proportion make himself an object of pity to men and, later in his life, repulsive to women. In this tragedy, as an inoffensive safety-seeker, he represents to the opposite sex, what the mouthy, entitled, policy-exploiting female does to the male; with the same outcome – rejection. So, the young boy who, misdirected by anti-bully programmes, fails to learn the lesson of the playground, also risks for the same reasons losing in the dating market. His female analogue, likewise misdirected to exploit pity to game the system for attention and advantage, risks the same. The hetero dating market is difficult enough without unwittingly adopting habits of thought that make one especially unattractive to the opposite sex. As the default initiator of romantic contact, this situation is especially damaging for a young man. We have seen many of these men, and heard even more of such women, in recent years. In both cases, never properly advised, with each failure they double down on the destructive behaviour, leading to increasingly sub-optimal choices and deeply felt failure; the women, bitter and militant and seen on marches against men; the men, sad and frustrated and unseen on the internet.

Everything here is about weakness; be safe, safe spaces, safe thoughts, everything safe seeking because everyone is apparently fragile. For every imaginary oppressor there is at least one victim group and, eventually, survivor group. Modernity, it seems, selects for weakness, but such a psychologically dubious safety must alter brain chemistry and contribute to the ongoing creation of a completely faggotised society, where whining and playing the victim increases your social status and bargaining power. Where the promise of a safe spaces for every conceivable type of person sounds great, but the reality of sub-contracting your security to the teacher, and later in adult life other agencies, is more than a disappointment. Where, too often, boys are undermined and the wrong girls energised. Teachers too are victims here, for they can unwittingly waste their entire careers trying to reconcile the anti-bully policy obligations with human nature. But they never will, for senseless garbage always prevails against logic. The longer they try, the stupider they will become.

Replacing the ad hoc method of managing bullying by policies that can be officially exploited will result in just such exploitation.

The anti-bully programmes are, then, just one other attack in the great and eternal war against us – a perfect concinnity of uselessness, hypocrisy and destroyer politics. In further stressing the school, it leads to projection of frustration onto others and, turning back on itself, causes more of the behaviour it is intended to address. It thus nicely complements the other elements of the harmful seven that put a headlock on our spirit and power of action. One may accept much of this argument, but believe that good intentions, perhaps misguided, lay behind the programmes. We accept this innocent view, but only at the operational level. At the deeper levels, I see a darker instinct at work here, and regard the presence of this and similar programmes as not an accident of badly aligned stars spoiling good intentions. For the end result is as was desired – the creation of victimarian identity politics to help break our hard-won social bonds and atomise us, all to better create the global nationless gulag. And what better way to promote this than encouraging a ratting and blame culture to make fragile and/or revengeful victim bots of our children; the next generation for the next generation of depression drug therapies[16] and nation destroying lawsuits. Someone is rubbing their hands at this – this is their heaven in our hell.

And then he said: *What are you going to do about it, eh?*

3
Charity

By walking to school we're collecting sponsorship money to buy a goat for husbandless African mothers with large families.[1]

Oh, that's nice. Here's 50p.

Introduction

What's Wrong With Helping Someone?

What Is Seen

The world is full of unfortunate others. Their condition is usually
deserving of pity and perhaps support. They are everywhere across
the globe and their numbers are ever increasing, as is their misery.
This is despite countless initiatives on our part, even including
that of our most powerful state agencies and celebrity ambassador
popteens. The putative kindness of the givers (us) is nearly always
highly visible by our own celebration of our giving. Especially
in schools:

£563.22 for AIDS babies in Somalia. WOW!!
Please share.

What Is Sometimes Seen

- A thinking person knows that not all charities scale up well.
  That what is worthy of support at face-to-face range in your
  own community becomes a different thing and more complex
  proposition when remote and global. It is this remote and global
  professional charity business that we are considering here.

- A thinking person knows that there is not much virtue in virtue
  signalling your charity, for by doing so you inadvertently reveal
  your real intent.

- A thinking person knows that often what we give is of no real
  value to us. Only the signalling is real![2]

- A thinking person knows that too many charity claims advanced too soon in life result in charity fatigue with claims routinely tuned out to the detriment of one's developing sympatico and ethical sense.

- A thinking person knows that Western largesse has resulted in little to no systemic difference and that tragically the final effect of our charity is often the opposite of the intention. And that this truth, although not at all hard to find, is kept from us.

- A thinking person knows that the cycle of deprivation has not been broken by Western promoted education and development, and will not be. And that solutions to poverty and misery have to come organically from the sufferers' own society.

- A thinking person knows that many charities have become businesses, and some of them negative forces for their original mission, so great is their inefficiency, hypocrisy, corruption and – above all-social damage to the host community. Thusly, they have reinforced the problems they were supposed to address.

- A thinking person knows that some types of charity must be finite otherwise they risk becoming dependence and a block to the dignity of independent development and, too, a catastrophic risk when lack of self-dependence meets (as it will) the hard time coming.

- A thinking person knows that the societal failure and beggary witnessed around the world has many causes with complex connections to us as Westerners, but in no fair way are we common people or our children to blame for this.

- A thinking person knows too that when we are referenced as complicit, or even directly responsible, for the plight of these ethnic-others, the actual 'we' is not us. But 'them'; that is, those who act for themselves under the false agency and cover of us. With us tricked to be included in their scheme as 'we'. 'Us' being who feels the guilt and takes the blame for the failures, and also pays for this, namely, you and I. 'Pays' meaning in every and any sense of the reckoning, money being the least cost to us. Although this 'least cost' is still gigantic!

However, despite the caveats, the thinking person would claim that we should do what we can to alleviate this suffering. We should do this because it is a moral injunction to help the needy, mandated by God and our inbuilt ethical coding. We should do it too because it creates a kinder, safer world for ourselves and our progeny. A further claim is that our progeny learn of, and strengthen, their virtues by being involved – if only this was promoted in schools. Now it is; so, win–win.

Perhaps.

What Is Not Seen

How this is actually presented in schools and who does this presenting; how a child processes this information and the long-term consequences to their understanding of the world and its problems, and especially their own emotional and simpatico development.

There is, of course, a reaction effect on the recipients of our charity, which is proportionally opposite to our efforts. Let the adults on the other end of the charity highway consider the effect on their societies and their children. Their charity too should begin at home.

Please note that we are not intending this argument to be an excursus on charity in general. Instead, we wish to focus on the effect on our children of our schools' charity initiatives. Also, we are not here referring to all charitable acts conducted on a child's independent account – assuming such a thing even exists anyway.

The View From Above

When visiting a primary school one often sees poster exhortations, class lessons and assembly references to charity. Implicit in this charity presence is the assumption that you really should care. Indeed, one could go further and conclude that a major purpose of our schools is to promote the moral need and iron-cast obligation on the part of our pupils to be always thinking about and acting for those limitless others requiring our patrimony. Too fanciful, think ye?

Children can't even enjoy playtime without being reminded of poverty, resurgent leprosy, their need to challenge lack of female rights – or whatever, dipped from the bucket list of Third World problems.

Until the last generation or so, schools showed no particular interest in supporting charities. Occasionally, there would be a suggested collection for something, perhaps involving some private interest of a staff member or a local connection to the school, but with no propaganda attached to the giving, nor shame to the not. Such activity was not regarded as in any wise part of the school's mission, and was in any case unnecessary, as churches and various organisations fulfilled this role as required. Thusly, no charity weeks, workshops, assemblies, fairs, videos, lesson reminders, parental involvement, shekel burning CPDs for teachers, and the whole school bent towards achieving some funding goal with contemptible celebrations and pious preening following. No big brother UN setting the goals and rewards – or rather, defining your fame or shame. Especially shame!

This situation changed as society changed. Firstly TV, then IT media, brought the misery of others in far-off, less-favoured, lands to dramatic focus; charitable organisations expanded to address this potential and a massive industry predicated on our strong and unique outgroup charitable impulse has developed. This includes the creation of a network of parasite and parastate institutions – e.g., think tanks, corporations, non-governmental organisations, and university research centres – all sucking off the public teat, and happy to stay so. Indeed, once established, practically impossible to get rid of. This, in turn, links as cause and effect to other societal trends to be later explored, but for the present, and for the purposes of moving on with this argument, we can hopefully accept as a great clash of fundamental values and future direction. This clash has segued from political discourse to social intercourse to school life and is heading towards the nursery; the protagonists recognising the crucial nature of creating future troops from our children for this societal battle against an enemy, ultimately identified through various iterations as White and European. Or, seen from the other end of the battlefield, the pupils' parents.

Charity in this argument is but one manifestation of the same Religion of Justice which wishes to remake our society by politicising our children.

The role of charity in this battle is to establish a set of obligations on our part to the needs of others, obligations which supersede any personal interest we may have in meeting those needs, and which are independent of reciprocity, or even self-interest. We are encouraged to believe such actions are indisputably good and right by themselves. These obligations have become conflated with social justice and, by playing upon the same charitable impulse, find themselves extended to other social justice ambitions currently active in schools; e.g., the sexualisation of children, racial guilt, tolerance, population replacement, various political and environmental projects. All these causes are actually expressions of the same globalist phenomenon and have the same cultural Marxist origins.

Charity, then, is another cannon in the assault on the walls of our children's well-being and our wealth.[3]

The endless charity projects fronted in schools begin this process of politicisation of our children under the guise of the good cause. The justification which underlies this pupil level of engagement with charity is childishly immature and based solely on what is presented in the media, but especially TV. However, there is a deeper level of political engagement that is generally kept hidden, and it is my contention that this is not innocent in its conception, nor in its intention towards our children – and it is this aspect that we shall explore in the rest of this chapter.

Whence Comes This Charity That Believeth and Hopeth All Things Good?

The charitable impulse has its origin in our rightful love of home and hearth, and for most societies throughout history it never strayed far, for obvious practical reasons and, more importantly, powerfully held family or tribal affinities which most definitely did not extend to outgroups – as a reading of the Old Testament will readily confirm. In this view, that someone not of your tribe or race is struggling with life is regarded as a good, as in realpolitik terms it manifestly is! Of course, it is well known for aid to be given to others, ostensibly on principle, but more likely for reasons of personal, political or dynastic advantage in the expectation of reciprocity. However, the charity tradition in the West could be argued as having a different starting impulse; that of an ideal derived from Christian universalism in practice. And it is from that same source that it derives its best benefit, for it is in the act of discrete giving and humble receiving that divine grace may enter our life. This can be as true for a child as an adult, and is independent of being a believing Christian. Crucially, though, this blessing is conditional on not intentionally pursuing it, or encouraging it with banal platitudes about kindness.

But when not powered by Christian piety or personal compassion, nor properly located at home and hearth, but obliged by diktat (as our schools' charity initiatives are) then, regardless of their merit, such charitable acts are not properly motivated by the moved spirit. Instead, they are acts of obeisance to the political world, and the demons of self-regard and social standing. Children's involvement is sullied by this.

Teaching hypocrisy: *Do what makes you look good.*

Irony fails when describing the contemporary charity champion who, having watched a TV advert, bravely fights against water poverty by searching the internet and posting a picture of a thirsty child with Faceborg link to a Justgive account – how insightful, how kind, how principled! ☺

Some children (usually girls) latch onto the possibilities of approval offered by charitable endeavours and by this means get an early start on the virtue signalling circuit. This precocious development takes their focus of societal concern away from home to duskier climes with duskier recipients. And dangerously, from the viewpoint of their own personal development, prioritises the approval of anonymous others who also ride the virtue signalling circuit. Thus early locking their opinions into the social media echo chamber and maximising the influence of media manipulations of their worldview.

Those children innocently seeking approval and status by this means can have no idea what they are involving themselves in; and especially the second, and successive, order effects to themselves and to their society – to say nothing of such impact on the recipient country's culture. They will never hear a reference to this hypothesis, far less a discussion; indeed, most adults have seldom considered such a thing either. And no censure is implied in noting that the ability to connect cause with effect through several orders of iteration is generally not a power held by primary school teachers. Their supposed good intention, as they understand it, can only have good effects. They just want to be seen as good people, and have no idea that they snared in a moral community manipulated by hostile overlords that control the entire panoply of sources of influence.

Proper charity, however, is too important a personal attribute to be hot-housed and become like a large, showy flower, but with a weak and false constitution.[4] It is a spiritual quality of the highest rank, indeed one of the seven Christian virtues, and is a crucial aspect of our society's success when properly expressed; this being to improve one's good affections and the proper disposition of the soul. It must be allowed grow in concordance with one's developing intellectual understanding of consequences and one's sympatico. For truly, compassion without wisdom, such as mistaken kindness unskilfully applied, inevitably has an evil outcome. The examples of this are legion, as are proverbs and saws proffering necessary advice. We should not be encouraging our children to turn into the sort of people who need the rest of us to believe that they are sacrificing for society, for this is a pathology.

Much Big Charity in the West has lost its virtue and become as if a branch of the entertainment industry,displaying itself variously in staged virtue signalling, infotainment with celebrities and, so-called, misery porn. Indeed, so relativist is our world, that even real porn is not left out, with charity becoming one of its subsets.[5] The dirty mind meets virtue signalling to their mutual benefit, when an apparently charitable impulse meets the global e-sex market; disentangle the degenerate societal tends and psycho-pathology that led us to that particular cesspool, if ye can! This, then, is just a part of the mind-deforming, entertainment hinterland that lies behind Big Charity. If Savile could return from his lake of boiling sulphur, he could tell us about that!

In the final analysis, Big Charity is just another racket.

Too often, then, 'doing charity' at school is reduced to just getting your face painted for 20p, pressuring parents for 'sponsorship' of worthless nothings and watching a video about poor kids; child slavery in Asia, Muslim girls with no dedicated skateboard park, or smiling, recently-fed Africans. After the self-celebration of the school's 'kindness and hard work' ☻ via an assembly video showing the same (aka, self-propagandising), the box gets ticked, the virtuous logo 'thank you' appears on the school website.[6] Now we forget about it, and wait on the next charity event to arrive on the guilt conveyer belt. There is seldom to never a follow-up regarding what really happened to the leveraged funds, or where the charitable initiative was known to be, frankly, a total failure; here, the whole thing just fizzles away to a forgotten nothing. What a life lesson; to have someone else define what you should care about, engage your emotional commitment, organise your involvement, take your money, help you feel good about this by means of some worthless token banner or the like, and then forget about it. No questions asked! *Really, don't ask them!*

From the veritable treasure cave of glittering nonsense we illustrate a most shining example of our school charity, which spectacularly involves giving something of even less worth than nothing; the Shoebox Santa. Here a well-meaning idiot had a beautiful vision of showing deprived African children how much Edinburgh children loved them, and how worthy she was of the attendant fame for conceiving such a gesture involving others. City education chiefs, keen to lap up some of the virtue cream that would splash around this project, naturally approved and so it went ahead to make an African Christmas to remember. City children were encouraged (i.e., shamed or otherwise forced) to fill a shoebox full of Christmas goodies – but, alas, no sweeties – mainly consisting of last year's discards, ugly cuddly toys,[7] story cassette tapes, burger restaurant colouring crayons, etc., basically capitalism's flotsam and jetsam. At enormous cost this was then collected and shipped in containers to sit for months at Dar es Salaam quayside before being driven upcountry to the recipient's garbage dump.

To the receiving children, such a gift box must have seemed like a psy-ops project and likewise to the perplexed militia leader, stopping the Christmas convoy for gunpoint tribute. We ask, how could the Santa box be thought of as anything other than an insult containing a debt? In my mind's eye, I imagine a child soldier, perhaps not so delighted with his box's contents, although the Pikachu figure could be used for target practice and the colouring-in crayons eaten as required. Whereas, no such practical use is likely to be found for the Thomas the Tank Engine dvd or clip-on donkey ears. We will return to the implications of such gestures to the recipient later in this argument.

But now meet Emmy;[8] her super power is charity. By seven years old she has saved scores of unfortunately parented others, both domestic and foreign domiciled. This has been done mainly by wearing face paint, dressing up or down and paying for the privilege, or scoring penalties against a teacher who, as her P7 brother noted with disappointment, just let the balls in (although, to be fair, he really was a rubbish goalkeeper). But, don't mock, she is learning how to save people far from her home. Once she collected nearly £5 for starving foreigners by selling self-bake muffins to schoolmates and teachers, although she later forgot to send the money to the charity as she candidly admitted.[9] But, aside from this memory slip, the effort is deemed worth it, and it pays itself back by the moral glow that this kindness gets from tweets and selfies. She has her own smart phone and so can blow her own i trumpet. The school UN flag is an added bonus which her mum was able to post as an online Christmas card: So Proud # Emmyloves. In real life, we know she hasn't given anything of value – except to herself and her mother. What a life lesson!

Mummy tweeted. Jesus wept.

Even before thinking of the real world destination and utility of our charity efforts, we can see in the 'gifts' themselves, ironic propitiation to those who caused the need for such in the first place, with their interference, and even destruction of the lives of foreign others, through political manoeuvring and economic witchery – or bombs, if required! True sympathy for the predicament of unfortunate others never extends to just leaving them alone – no ruinous economic interference, no World Banks 'loans', no creation of Western-dependent elites, no regime change, no sponsoring Western golems, no 'delivering democracy', no drone strikes![10] But instead, we demonstrate empathy for the world's disadvantaged by working within paradigms created and managed by the organisations that that have caused the problems, and supporting them through the financial and political bureaucracies that maintain this. One could come to the belief that, rather than eradicating poverty and need, the true goal of Western charity is the provision of endless Western charity.

And while we go along mindlessly being shamed or manipulated by those with their own agenda, they secretly smile at our moral grandstanding, knowing that thusly do we prove their mastery over our worldview and our emotional life. And too, as a part of this process, we have been taught to throw our nation's wealth and our personal monies into a huge money pit on encouragement of the claimed good cause, without thinking of the consequences, or shamed to silence if we do. Our psychological conditioning in respect of this has created a charity juggernaut which will eventually overwhelm us. 'They' must delight in the feedback loop that schools have developed between parent and pupil, each reinforcing in familial competition the undermining of the Western family as a future presence in the world by means of toxic altruism planted by the deceptively harmless looking seed of charity.[11]

Demonic mission achieved; our kindness turned against ourselves with our schools the incubator of this fever and female teachers the vectors. Their mothering instinct, easily transferred to needy creatures and causes, especially beautiful brown babies, finds sympathetic concurrence in the school's charity-focused outlook and projects. Indeed, this entire phenomenon is totally dependent on the institution being feminised, as the female need to herd think within the dominant trope enforces the charity orthodoxy. Here, a question posed in the staffroom provides a challenge to one's integrity; answer honestly and face the anger of these janissaries of the New World Order, or dissemble and survive:

So, you're in favour of [select Third World country] *children having their legs blown off by mines and then starving to death?*

Well, frankly,…oh, look! The sun's came out at last.

True Compassion Is a Consequence of Spiritual Growth

In the development of personality, each attribute should come in its own time and with its proper motivation. A genuine concern for the world is just such an attribute, and whatever charitable expression flows from this is too important to a child's development for it to be forced.

In an ideal world, the lives of children would be carefree. They would develop at their own pace and in their own way to be who they were meant to be. As loving adults we would oversee this process, preventing them from harm both physical and mental. We would ensure that they were exposed to the ideas and experiences appropriate to their level of development. This development has two components of relevance to us here; emotional and intellectual. It is my contention that the charity project violates this by introducing topics and concerns which the children are not yet equipped to understand. And, in particular, their own role in whatever concern they are exposed to. Children's thinking processes are egocentric, whatever they see is processed as linked to them in some causal way. With respect to charity, this is understood as an obligation on them and, by extension, their family and community. They cannot, we adults can (although we often do not), rationalise this feeling and allocate it a proper place in our priorities, and then decide for ourselves a level of involvement appropriate to that. We might even be aware of manipulation, and even deceit, in this process. The child, presented with an adult sponsored project (this includes UN, EU, etc., as proxy adults) has no real option of deciding for themselves their level of interest or involvement. It's a form of bullying.

The child, then, experiences much of this charity propaganda as blame. Even if they do not care about the cause or even understand it, this attitude itself still contains the potential for blame. In this case, a double whammy of blame for not caring about not caring; for even indifference carries a cost! If in silence, the cost of internalising feelings and, perhaps, supressing expression. If the indifference is expressed aloud, the child in question is likely to receive a verbal rebuke, most probably from female classmates– as I have witnessed. This child unwittingly receiving an early demonstration of the female 'point and shriek' outing he will receive as an adult should he attempt to inject some scepticism into this debate, or indeed, any debate that opposes herd-think orthodoxy.

By attempting to force sympathy and compassion on our children, without regard to their age or sex, we are distorting the natural development of these forces and by this corrupting them. A seven-year-old boy is not like an eleven-year-old girl, and yet both are considered as equals in the presentation of charity propaganda. The only thing they both understand equally is that only the native White children are targeted, the ethnic-others also know this across their entire age range. In the assembly hall watching the video of ragged begging street-children transformed to smiling trainee engineers and doctors by Western charity, the five year old has no idea what they are watching, whereas the eleven year old perfectly understands the guilt given to them, although not the true motive.

Our children's lives are full of enough worries, without assaulting their minds further with images of misery derived from charity appeals. You cannot just repeatedly slide such tales of woe and need onto a child's plate and expect there to be no consequences in their understanding of the world and their own place in it. The professionally produced misery porn to which children are exposed is designed to elicit the response it does. From a marketing viewpoint it is brilliantly done, in that it forever changes the target's perceptions and preferences. The germ of guilt and race responsibility does not go away after the sponsorship money is handed in. This guilt is surely a part of the mental health crisis among our children.

Another aspect of charity seldom considered is its closeness to contempt, both emotions occupying the same territory and separated by a very hazy no-man's land of indifference. It does not take much for enthusiastic compassion to become fatigued, and for this to segue into indifference and then contempt. The endless nature of the charity initiatives in school and the compulsion to be, not just involved, but to celebrate too, eventually must drive out pity. And then turn it toxic, as this charity fatigue must be publicly hidden and privately repressed. The child well understands this power, even as they cannot express it. Our charity initiatives ironically creating their opposite; here, then, we see illustrated a nice model of second order effects mocking our lack of wisdom.

Let your child live their life and grow into a compassion that is proper for them.

Awake ye parents and intelligent pupils! Masked as charity, this moral grandstanding does not connect to our Christian sensibility and mission, which alone would justify the forced involvement of children. Without God in this equation, the act is secular, just one group giving another, via anonymous all-White agencies, creating a debt that need not be repaid under God's auspices, but most certainly will without. When the giving is not a true act of charity properly inspired, the recipient becomes a dependent, cynically gaming the largesse and eventually resentful anyway. However Whites consider charity, the rest of the world does not see it that way, viewing it instead as tribute from the cowardly, or reparations from the guilty.

The Good Samaritan:
A Parable To Die For

Feeding off the vestigial remains of Christianity, the parable of the good Samaritan gets wheeled out to illustrate, by his compassionate example, Jesus's endorsement of the principle of charity to others. This appeal to the highest authority is usually delivered once a year by the minister in their yearly circuit of the diocese schools. Although, given the level of Christian religious belief, its acceptance and re-use by teacher atheists is somewhat hypocritical, nonetheless it cannot be gainsaid, as religion here conveniently serves the given narrative of *Give*.

As it is presented in schools, its message is simple and clear, apparently; but actually, not. The parables are full of meaning, most of it unstated, to be discovered by study, discussion, prayer and reflection. Jesus's parables too often have the context ripped out, as in the case of the good Samaritan. This story is no longer one which illustrates Christian piety in action, but globalist politics.

This is not the place for exegesis as to the various interpretations of this parable except to note that the Samaritan helped a single person in immediate need and with his own time and money. He did not oblige a government agency to do this deed, nor press the charity button at the checkout, nor arrange for the injured man's family to be sent to the Samaritan's home village to be permanently housed there at the villager's cost, nor send funds abroad (via global banking cartels) to feel virtuous and boast about it via Twitter. The Samaritan's actions were small scale and personal; the proper focus for charity. And had no effect on his own, or the victim's, home society.

Whatever you did for the least one of these brothers of mine, you did also for me. Too often, though, the charitable donation is nothing of value. And nothing of value, added to hypocrisy and moral preening, is less than nothing. Jesus knows the difference. It's the opposite of the widow's mite.

> *It is a gracious ambition to covet to be really more holy than others, but it is a proud ambition to covet to appear so. It is good to excel in real piety, but not to exceed in outward shows; for overdoing is justly suspected of design.*
>
> Proverbs. 27:14

You see, God knew your heart all along!

Donor Group and Recipient Group:
Always the Same

Here we posit that the essential nature of the Act of Charity as it is mandated in our schools is, in fact, an act of power that corrupts on either side of the outstretched hands.

We may believe that in promoting charity in schools we are *only* doing good, but how does it feel on the other end of the charity highway; to always be the recipient? How would the adults involved over there in [select Third World country] rationalise this situation; with endless gratitude, think ye? How is their need for foreign charity explained to their children? Is it explained, or even considered at all? Why always the recipient, why endlessly pathetic? Do they become prickly in their beggary, as we might in our ethnic pride? Do they resent even the *thought* that they are perhaps regarded as the playthings of a capricious god, or as parasites on an alien race's largesse? And what role can the never-ending, global-wide narrative of White racism, as the go-to explanation for any issue involving non-Whites, play in their understanding of their circumstances, except to legitimise victimhood and ingratitude.

However, any gratitude we may imagine is our due has actually never flipped, because it never existed in the first place; the money shot pictures of smiling beggar children notwithstanding. The subjects of the posters know their own history as one of grievances against White empire, or just Whites in general – and in this thought they are admirably encouraged by cabal-owned global media.

At the visceral level, the recipient understands the nature of the gift and the alien race power displayed. Likewise their ranking in the scheme of things; Whitey again, with the power and them with the need. Whitey always do-gooding, sanctimonious and superior, but guilty for his slavery, his colonial theft, his racism and cruelty; this reinforced every day by global English MSM and celebrity UN ambassadors for White guilt. What develops, then, is an intuitive understanding that White charity is buying the favour of their gratitude, the purchased indulgence for the religion of our time, White guilt. A truth sarcastically recognised as such by ingrate recipients; Whatever White society does can never be enough to assuage the anger of such true racists. The Children see Stormzy getting his award on TV and then lambasting British Whites as racist in his acceptance speech; ingrate gratitude, lack of self-restraint and irony all perfectly illustrated.

Considering our children, what do they make of this state of affairs: Why are the receivers always Black and Asian? Why don't their own parents look after them?[12] Why doesn't their own government fix their problems? Why are the problems never solved despite all our charity initiatives? Children are seldom able to consider these questions in the direct manner framed here, however, their tacit understanding of these queries fills the interstices between their knowledge and instinct. The real reason why Ajeed is homeless, Shavanni is a slave or little Achekwi has to walk five miles to collect dirty water could be explained, likewise why their mummies and daddies don't look after them, but really cannot be and will not be.

Also understood by our children, as if coming with the charity bundle, is the enforced silence that invariably attends adult consideration the same topics. This sense not to ask such questions is the starter lessons for the White adult requirement to say nothing suggestive of even slight scepticism when issues involving the doubly explosive mixture of charity and race are publicly discussed.

That proxy representatives of foreign domiciled charity recipients are likely to be present in most schools renders free speech to us mannerly natives almost impossible.

Children may not yet have the vocabulary, but dependency and parasitism, playing the system and feeling guilt are animal attributes well understood at that level. People don't like owing a debt which cannot be paid back, but on the other hand, people don't like ingratitude; each rationalises as best suits themselves. This goes for children too. Unanswered queries, unspoken resentments, confusions, irresistible social pressures, distressing stories and images, never-ending want, guilt, hidden to fester until the time to find an outlet. Hegel's cunning of reason proven.

What we are now seeing has been termed pathological altruism in action. And discovering that, masked as charity and allied with claims of fairness, justice and compassion, these are all plays on our emotions. This is a complex of forces whose end intent is our ruin. 'Charity' is just another anti-White hustle. Only Whites are susceptible to this agenda, other ethnicities understand intuitively that self-preservation provides limits to outgroup compassion; which are often by default set to zero. This is as Nature intended, and is a proper and honest setting with which to discuss topics of mutual interest between various groups and upon which, freed from fawning, to discover that which you admire in the other.

Our ancestral fathers knew the truth of this; continually mitigating the plight of an unknown other only serves to make them HATE YOU.

The truth is White Charity has only ever had one child, and his name is Black Resentment.

Reluctantly, even to the point of shame or self-deception, but inevitably one arrives spiritually exhausted at the only destination of this pilgrim's road; the ultimate attitude – *I don't care!*

As seen on a classroom door:

AN AFRICAN FARMER GETS JUST 50P A DAY FOR GROWING YOUR CHOCOLATE.

EVERY DAY A CHILD DIES FROM DRINKING DIRTY WATER.

WHAT'S YOUR FAVOURITE COLOUR? MEERA LOVES YELLOW. DON'T LET MEERA GO BLIND! FOR 50P YOU CAN HELP HER AND GIVE THE GIFT OF SIGHT.[13]

The world's problems are not their fault of our children and they should not be exposed to them as they currently are. Parents need to help their children to escape from the endless guilt, endless responsibility, endless hate circle into which too much charity is immersed.

It might be hoped that in its strong sweep through schools, this charity mania will exhaust its febrile power, but such is the nature of this hex that such an outcome is not in the foreseeable future and so it falls to the parents, if they so wish, to introduce their child to some ugly realities regarding how charity segues to dependence to parasitism to resentment to revenge, and how they should not feel guilt. And that there is not just hidden complexity and ironies and hypocrisies in the charity drive, but hidden intent against them.

Their parents need to keep them away too from damaging virtue signalling, especially with social media. They need encouragement to see through social justice and compassion claims. They need to be taught the sources of such brainwashing and learn to ignore it with:

I don't care!

They need to be taught the old wisdom, don't do too much for someone. Eventually they resent it. And, anyway it will not bring you insurance against being called a racist

Lastly, they need to know that they will earn no grace or favour at that final judgement for their highly visible, attention-seeking goodness. Such behaviour is the opposite of charity, and he who knows, knows.

Why Is This Happening?

If charities have become the playthings of a long game, ultimately against us. Who is the shadowy 'they' who stands behind this social project and secretly smile at our moral grandstanding? Do they even exist?

Clearly, this is not just a plot. Historical forces below the level of consciousness slowly drive the public mind to create the zeitgeist, the spirit of the times. Here, the big wheel of history turns and lands in the West with a focus on social justice, on equity, on universal brotherhood and fixing everyone's problem; formerly known, in colonial times, as the White man's burden, but reborn in our times as Western guilt and blame. This aspect has something of the madness of crowds, especially amplified in institutions that strongly feature women. Remembering the adage, those whom the gods want to destroy, they first make mad:

Where are all you girls going?

Over the cliff. It's for charity.

Hey, great. Can I come?

However, everywhere when examined in depth, the zeitgeist reveals the hand of the master. The real advocates are not who you see proselytising for the cause, either earnest spokesmen or popworld-idiot celebrities. Nor are they the assorted racketeers and race-hustlers attracted like flies to the stench of dirty project money with which the charity world is awash. Not the political activist and guilt-mongers for multiculturalism, although they are in on it, as foreign charity initiatives help keep the guilt level high. Neither are they the people who make the professionally produced videos and other misery porn promo, they just work for money, although some of this latter group, knowing that they are dealing in emotional manipulations and less than truths, must be party to the plan and brushing sleeves with 'them'; and thusly a degree beyond being a dupe and shading into 'willing executioner' zone.

This 'them' is risky to name, and this situation is not an accident. If your intent is to destroy a people you'd want to remain in the background, create legal protection and use proxies, at least until you didn't need to. Which is how it will be, as it has been.

Their actions are almost instinctive as they are based on a hatred of us that has ancient roots seldom examined, and often illegal to do so anyway. Using their ownership of the MSM, the entertainment industry, global publishing and influence in academia, they have turned our open society and its essential kindness against ourselves by the reinforcement of false histories and guilt-inducing narratives. In the confusion of this programming, by dint of seeking a psychological balance, we try harder to be good and encourage the same among our children; unwittingly, by doing so, making ourselves into golems – creatures who do their masters bidding, but with no understanding of why. Some have become so well-programmed that the resulting self-hatred can only find solace in the most vigorous advocacy of outgroup others; even should those others openly blame and visibly hate them – such toxic feedback being like oxygen to their sick minds.

It is these activist-advocates, operating within the charities and their related legal advocacy and political/media influences, that have created, over generations of supposed do-gooding, the Malthusian tidal wave of desperate and ingrate others that threatens the West and stresses native home countries throughout the world. 'They' want this. And while they own the world, this international charity madness, and the self-scouring mindset that accompanies, it will never end.

To get the names of these Tikkun Olams and Goody Two Shoes, either institutional or individual just, as mentioned before, follow the funding and advocacy backwards; policy by policy, manipulated report after report, funded project by funded project, celebration by celebration and we are led to the vipers den. The same names, the same people, every single time. They won't be happy until...

Tying It Up

See, good reader, the connection between charity and the wider assault on our children's welfare:

- how 'charity' as a political concept is spread by powerful media voices preaching White guilt, often from a Christian perspective,

- and how school charity initiatives depend on the daily priming of the mind by the delivery of endless tragedy via media news, reinforced in class by BBC *Newsround*,

- and how the whole charade is conducted under the auspices of the UN which further legitimises itself by providing rewards to the compliant,

- all of which feed the institutional charity monster which perpetuates the problem abroad and enables race guilt and resentment at home,

- by creating a backdrop of misery involving others,

- but connected to us by an apparently inescapable obligation, which feeds the tacit assumption of a world somehow damaged or made unjust by us,

- which reinforces the concepts and language of bitterness and self-hatred, volubly denied – but by this denial, quietly confirmed – by false and forced multicultural celebrations,

- while politicising our children and crushing dissent by social pressure,

- that creates the mental confusion that leads our children to their immiseration and their culture to denigration and, by lacking champions, easy replacement.

All the qualities which, in our own world free from nefarious intent on us, we should value, have instead become the infection vectors for our society: Diversity, tolerance, kindness, multiculturalism and respect, all conspire to damage our social immune system, replacing rational self-interest with guilt and servility. Conformity, too, is more than encouraged, as any who express any doubts about 'our values – charity' soon finds out; and here our children learn by example, the mockery of free speech and its replacement by self-enforced censorship.

And, our educational goal, the global citizen, becomes an own-goal! In this jaundiced view, charity is the plucking of the heartstrings that confuses the judgement with emotion.

As a Head teacher noted, alas, a little too late:

HT to God: *We thought we were raising the enlightened child of the 21st century. We thought we were doing our part in setting the history record straight. We didn't think it through, honestly. We didn't know what we were doing to our own children. The pictures were very sad and we wanted to help. We never thought of long-term effects, no one ever mentioned them. We just joined the charity bandwagon, all the other schools were doing it and we wanted a nice UN flag too. We just didn't know what we were doing. Honestly, we didn't really think about it. We just didn't know!*

God to HT: ***Well, ye know now!***

I am optimistic that this breathless incantation will show that charity in schools is indeed part of the cultural Marxist programme, and that we are walking our children into a trap, and with them our society. It is our cultural naivety and basic kindness of heart, rather than just stupidity that helps keep a more based view of charity from public consciousness. For us ethnic Whites, moral communities, rather than kinship, are the social glue of our Western societies. And as such, one's main concern is to have a good reputation in that community which is now defined, not by the actual community an individual resides in, but by the media and the educational system. These are implacably hostile to any expression of White self-interest, this includes awareness of toxic altruism and the associated resistance to faux charity. This situation is regrettable, but cannot be otherwise until a new type of White person emerges that has regard for the future of their own bloodlines. And who will, like Caesar to his soldiers, say:

Those that hate me, I will learn to loathe.

It is apparently not enough simply to live our lives as good people in our own families and communities, we must somehow justify our existence beyond earning a living and paying our taxes. Here we call time on this claim on our charity. Love your own.

Sympathy is not to be commanded.[14]

HARDENING

4
BBC *Newsround*

Preparing Children for Entry to the 24/7 Popworld

Introduction

More Screen Time in the Global Digital Playground; Just What Our Children Need

In two generations TV news has become an indispensable part of British cultural and family life, an astonishing transformation of the domestic setting and our habits.[1] For this reason the subject matter of my argument inevitably spills over to cover a wider area, for our family life is now, literally, lived partly in another realm – the digital one. It would thus seem to be futile to frame this argument in terms that were critical of the majority of families and their stewardship of their children with respect to TV; however, such a criticism seems impossible to avoid, as the points that build our particular argument regarding the school's role in intentionally exposing children to mainstream media news, in the form of BBC *Newsround*, equally apply to all of us.

Intelligent adult viewers understand that TV is exponentially self-discrediting itself and that, in conjunction with the mobile phone, excess dietary sugar and social media, is rewiring our brains incorrectly. In accepting this understanding of TV, I am thus optimistic that parents will be able to consider this argument against BBC *Newsround* (hereafter referred to as plain *Newsround*) without feeling it as a personal criticism of their viewing habits.[2]

Our BBC: it was once believed as a byword for truth and the standard by which to measure other countries' news media. Of course, it always served its master's agenda, but that being, as we considered it, essentially traditional and establishment made its perspective on events seem much like our own; trying to be reasonable, modestly British. And too, we generally accepted that the 'old school' boys that managed the news services were fundamentally decent in character and committed to fairly reporting events. With respect to TV news, this approach was reactive and carried no deliberate attempt to drive a separate and radical agenda, far less create a new mindset. No doubt, this description reflects an idealised Britain and is rosier than the reality of those far-off days when, in actuality, TV news always had a low percentage of honest content value. This eulogy of old-time TV news may be exaggerated, but one thing is certain, no such eulogy could be honestly made for the BBC news now.

This comparison between then and now is becoming increasingly noticed, and the BBC is dividing its viewers like never before. This is especially so with respect to the various cultural issues which form the subjects considered in this book. Indeed, many viewers have come to regard BBC news as a prime source of manipulating misinformation and a driver of the dystopia we increasingly witness. This latter point leads us to *Newsround*, the BBC's daily news programme for children, regularly watched in our primary schools, typically post playtime. Like regular TV news, which has accelerated to propaganda hyperdrive within a decade, *Newsround* too has made the transition to cultural agitprop. The earlier times when children were not regarded as appropriate recipients, far less targets, for news, and indeed were generally protected from such, is well past.

Watched every day, the same topics repeated with the same tacit assumptions by the same quacky-voiced multicultural crew, acting out the gamut of prescribed emotions, from breezy to doleful, calibrated to elicit the 'proper' emotional response to the news item in question, *Newsround* becomes a powerful force in the life and worldview of a child. Most adults agree that the giant cache of digital banality that constitutes TV life and news is downsizing their mind; consider the same on the unformed mind of your child.

The evil triumvirate that lives in BBC *Newsround*; agitprop, UN mandates and celebrity culture.

We should be protecting our children from this, but instead school management leads the betrayal by heedlessly promoting *Newround*; idiotically believing that by such they are encouraging the development of the informed and activated global pupil so beloved by our Scottish curriculum.

Class teachers go along with this mandate mostly because they agree with it, and partly for the lazy convenience (or frightful necessity) of ten free minutes to sort themselves for the next lesson, while their charges yet again find themselves looking at a screen.[3]

Once more in our arguments in this book we enter into the world of what is seen and what is not seen. There are three issues to be considered regarding children's exposure to TV news in school; the principle, the content and the effect.

The Principle

Whose Child Is It Anyway?

The first issue is the simplest of points; do you want your child watching TV news in school? If you approve of this particular form of extra screen time in class without reservation, then the issue is concluded. *You may leave early!*

If, however, you hold reservations of any nature and believe that, as the parent, you should choose if your child is to be connected to the news matrix in school – for the children themselves are given no choice about this – then you owe it to your own conscience to examine *Newsround* for content suitability and editorial intent. And too, consider the potential for the teacher led discussions that can, and are often encouraged to, take place afterwards, segueing to endorsing the, possibly young and likely female, opinion of the teacher herself. Such opinions on typical topics can be fairly reliably guessed to be the same as her peers. This, then, is the principle in question activated.

It could be logically contended that, as parents have entrusted their child's education to their school, then those same parents must be in broad agreement with the curriculum's content and methodology. And this includes the use of *Newsround* as a means of meeting the global activist goals that are clearly posted on every school website and endlessly referred to in official educational communications. Notwithstanding the general truth of this contention, default delegation to schools for the management of our children's education does not forfeit the right to action over worrying specifics.

Such a right to challenge this, or indeed any other, feature of the curriculum is described by school policy. Far be it, though, for school management to kindly grant this concession and your local education authority to be its guarantor, for such a right to your child's welfare has an irrevocable pedigree, that of blood and sacred duty. Only God's rights to your child may be considered to stand above this, despite the competing claims of the Scottish government's 'better than God' attempt to transfer such rights legally to the professional scrutiny of a social worker, or some other equivalent functionary of the state.[4] My blood still boils at the thought of this!

This right is further justified in this age of fake news by a real concern for the quality and impartiality of the journalists collating, and even manufacturing, the news. The death of independent and trustworthy journalism is real, and *Newsround* does not appear out of the aether unsullied by this fact. One may respond that the BBC is publicly owned and is therefore not beholden to the mega-corporations that drive the global agenda and, by not requiring advertising revenues, escapes from this controlling power. However, the BBC operates in the same media hinterland as its commercial cousins, ultimately relying on the same conveyor belt of staged events, fake scripted heroes and villains, manipulated emotions and false hopes, scrolling through Twittterland harvesting its own planted items and feeding the controversies it has created. All the while, sharing with its erstwhile rivals the same media-establishment attitudes to unfavoured topics, and crushing references to no-go subjects and the truths that can never be spoken.[5]

The BBC's position in this respect is further complicated in that it acts as a player in this global game, trading off its legacy in the marketing of its commercial products through independent divisions. In actuality, then, the BBC is a fully functioning and fully willing part of the global TV and news matrix. And for this reason, then, just watching *Newsround* contributes to the legitimisation of all TV news as a source of reference and opinion, arguably even *the* source. In the case of the child watching *Newsround*, this legitimisation receives the further authority of the teacher's approval by the mere fact that they are watching it in class. This basic acceptance of the world picture created by TV news is not affected by any particular news items, no matter how uninteresting, trivial or deceitful. And likewise, as a principle, this argument is not affected by *Newsround* topics that are content neutral or interesting to a child. The end effect is the same: TV news and TV life receives a tacit endorsement which the children implicitly understand: the TV, it endlessly affirms, is where you find out about the world.

And our children are prepped for accepting endless TV news in the rest of their lives. And this they will get without mercy! Everywhere they go they will find TV news as a default background; superstores, medical surgeries, chip shops, bars, waiting areas, buses, and carried 24/7 on mobile phones. TV is normal and TV is good, a child must instinctively think this; how could they think otherwise?

No news is good news.

One may argue that the child is not forced to watch the news, and even though they are not given an active choice about this (such as giving those who do not wish to watch it permission to leave the classroom and/or do something else), they are free to ignore it – as children easily do with lessons when they are not engaged with them. However, ignoring a large, centrally placed screen with compelling moving images is not an easy option, as any adult who has been in a pub knows. To do so takes great willpower, and especially so when the images are dedicated to children's interests. (e.g., 'We report on the premier of the new Star Wars', 'Sad news for panda lovers', or 'The British man taking up Greta's challenge of cutting down on global warming by wearing the same unwashed undercrackers for six months').[6] Further, there is often a follow-up discussion or lesson based on the news item, and so the child's attention is obligated. Practically, then, the child, your child, is forced to watch TV news whether they want to or not.

Our curriculum mandates that our children should be informed about the world, and most parents would of course agree with this ambition. But doing so, I believe, in ignorance of what their children are often being informed about and the intent of those doing the informing. For example; should, or even can, a child at seven years old have an informed opinion on same sex marriage, fat shaming, transgender athletes, BLM, Third World water poverty, or be presented on Robert Mugabe's death with an overview of his life? Should any of the topics they study in class be connected to TV news and more screen time? Should children be exposed to child campaigners as role models, when we know there are exploiting adults operating such campaigners as puppets? Should media celebrities, with their vast manipulative power, be allowed to show their dissembling faces (and skimpy costumes, if female) in class, as if they are role models for anything of proper value?[7]

Thusly, being 'informed' may not be the universal good it may at first appear; particularly when there is a complete failure, as is the case with *Newsround* , to control content for the age range of its target audience. i.e., P3s are not like P7s, and yet both watch the same TV news in class.

Most people have no need for constant TV news at all; indeed, they have far greater need for protection from it. If the MSM news were occasional and genuine, one could argue for its legitimate purpose in a democracy. However, it is now a propaganda delivery service cataloguing degeneracy, dysfunction and misery. We are drinking in this news as if from a hosepipe, and being informed all the way to confusion, misery, and even to depression.

Given this situation, we ask; should TV news be part of our children's school day? Is this not priming them for the television without mercy that has led us adults and our society to the bleak land of too much life lived looking at a rectangle? Or, put another way, have they not got better things to be doing than watching the TV again?[8]

The Content

The News Is Not Real News, and the Real News Is Not Spoken Of At All

The intent of *Newsround* is the same as that of any other mass media news outlet; manufacturing consent for its agenda, which is that of its global investment group owners. This may seem to have been complicated somewhat by the fact that we, the British public, are the owners of the BBC. However, as we have alluded to above, in the real world, our ownership is putative and we are merely the involuntary funders, for the BBC is well and truly 'owned' by those who are responsible for its form and content. And that's not us.

This agenda is revealed by the content, which is the same as the BBC adult news, but cleverly (or rather, fiendishly!) calibrated to child level. Indeed, as it is designed to appeal to unformed minds, one finds as an adult watching *Newsround* that it more clearly demonstrates its manipulations and its agenda, in comparison to its adult equivalent. Hopefully, the parental examination of *Newsround* on behalf of their child may lead those same adults to a better awareness of the hostile power behind the news and thus begin their own detoxification from this rectangle of mind death.

Newsround is easily available to parents to assess its content themselves. They will notice that a truly gigantic and thoroughly professional effort is put into the daily delivery of *Newsround* and also that their website is enormous and clearly (frighteningly so!) well-funded. This is no second-string, budget kiddie's show. Like us adults, our children too are drinking news from a hosepipe.

Viewed neutrally, they will find it especially concerned with manufactured child news items, entertainment trivia, spurious surveys, the opinions of juveniles and poptart celebrities, product placement,[9] climate change, human rights, plucky and/or struggling children in Africa and Asia, man-made disasters, the plight of unfortunate others, new IT apps and games (these are always cool), apparent prejudice confronted and the fantastic achievements of child activists. But especially, the BBC's reflex topics, sex and race; best summarised as minority worship and female empowerment. Many of the features radiate this obsession like background uranium, invisible to the innocents, but poisoning their minds just the same. And all presented with a funky soundtrack and chirpy, teeny, box-ticking, actor-presenters who are, like their adult equivalents, 100% talking haircuts.

Judged for what it is, it is expertly produced garbage; but as propaganda, brilliant.

Misery is another *Newsround* staple. Here they will find sensitive (or attention-seeking) children supposedly accommodated by warnings to look away at an upcoming report's disturbing images (child refugees, maltreated pets, children who suffer from…, etc.) and this sensitivity (or attention seeking) further addressed by helpline numbers; thus subtly alerting children how to process the info and evince the 'correct' sympathetic – and frankly, girly – response. Thereby contributing to the encouragement of a faux 'full retard' sensitivity like Greta T's; her potential emulators, children themselves, seeing the social credit to be enjoyed by displaying a sympathy so apparently profound that it hurts them.

Checking the comments section on the *Newsround* website reveals children dutifully posting back the opinions just fed to them – so achievement unlocked as regards propagandised! The ability to comment is, of course, only available where they can be certain of the 'correct' opinion being expressed. Typically, one sees the 'One world, love all' type of message posted; the same diversity and tolerance virtue signalling one finds with their adult form. Indeed, *Newsround* should be thought of as training for this – and an excellent example of human programming!

As with advertising and sports, once again we see the political world intruding into another domain; this time the target is our children.

A parent checking *Newsround* will find that their children are regularly introduced to ideas and terms regarding intolerance and bigotry and societal dysfunction. Typically these are interwoven into factual reports or child interest features. Such stories are global in scope, but the inevitable focus of blame eventually (if only by implication) winds its way back to us ethnic Whites. The factually disingenuous presentation of such issues as a problem in the first place is simply first level propaganda, and no honest understanding will be achieved by children. This, of course, is irrelevant to the propagandists. Their only interest is to inject into our children the tropes of the unjust society and global village. The same promulgated everywhere you look in the adult world. Namely; the nation-killing lie!

In contrast, they will never find celebration of native British culture for its own sake, although they might find it referenced as a bait and switch for the multiculturalism that they actually wish to celebrate (the refugees who are learning Welsh or Somali pupils Morris dancing, etc.). And by this avoidance, tacitly denying a White identity or interest. In contrast, multiculturalism will be relentlessly celebrated, either by inference as an approved backdrop to some activity, or directly by an adult authority figure leading the celebration – for example, a head teacher 'proudly' celebrating that her school has 33 languages spoken in it, without saying what is actually worth celebrating about that, or noting the cost in British shekels for supporting this Babellian bazaar. They will never find boys and girls celebrated for themselves, but only as representatives of political interest, for example breaking sex barriers with respect to some activity, with the tacit assumption that cross gender competition or colonisation of each sex's particular interests is meritorious by itself. The upshot of this absence of a native cultural touchstone is to subtly pathologise European normality, or more rather, what that was until recently!

However, the ultimate 'No-no!' as regards celebration is that of parenting and its corollary of success, the happy family. The good mother and father in a stable ethnic White British family is as never existed. One may wonder why this is, particularly when struggling parents (ideally, Third World and single female) often feature as a lead into a child-focused report. It seems that certain types of traditional families evoke the wrong associations for *Newsround*'s purposes.

A common *Newsround* strategy is using feature reports as advocacy for its approved causes; for example, 'More schools are setting up food banks', 'A great new app that lets you track the migrant caravans live', 'Why are more families becoming vegan', 'A school in [select] is doing its bit to save [select]', etc. Such always involves an expert authority, typically young and ideally a celebrity. Of course, the expert is more likely to be just a PR mouthpiece for their funded and owned advocacy 'research' group. The style and script of such coverage leaves the watching pupil with no problem discerning what the proper opinion is, as well as holding out to them an advocacy template which not only garners adult approval, but also receives the attention of TV. And for many children – *As Seen on TV* – is the ultimate level of approval. In this way, *Newsround* reinforces the explicit notion that school should be a place where you fight for political issues under the guise of social justice.

Almost everything in *Newsround* is subsumed to politics. This is the very definition of totalitarian thinking, and only the funky, colourful nature of its presentation disguises the internal frenzy of this vision.

With respect to this advocacy aspect, I am particularly aggrieved at the use of falsely claimed child achievements as emotional levers against normal children with normal interests that do not include a fashionable social cause. Although the children who watch such age-peer avatars cannot know this, every adult who watches understands the very high level of parent/adult//PR consultant involvement and appreciates how disingenuous such child advocacy usually is; and, too, that the parental involvement as tout often has ambition levels that can exceed the restraints of discretion and family love. That many children have been mentally ruined by parents using their child as a front for *their* ambition and desire for recognition is, of course, never mentioned.

A related advocacy strategy is the use of spurious surveys of pupil opinion. Their ridiculous level of fictionality and the transparent nature of their manipulation reveals the focused intent of those behind such strategies, for this is not an example of shoddy practice or even of ignorance in action, but a deliberate attempt to coerce pupil opinion by appealing to their social need to participate and conform. *The results from the survey of* **your** *opinion of having same sex couples on Britain's Dancing Bake Off are in. Let's take a look…*

Higher order thinking leads behind the content to consider the unchallenged assumptions underlying them, together with the ignored news and eliminated opinions, as the seeds of a future mindset; for example:

1. That children should know about the topics *Newsround* choses to cover and that this is a good thing.

And the topics and perspectives it doesn't cover are not worthy of attention, and that this too is a good thing. And too, the topics not mentioned may even be bad (as bad, even, as racist or sexist!) and would lead pupils to the wrong conclusion. That TV news is a legitimate source of disinterested information on the world and that any authority figures introduced, e.g., celebrity UN ambassadors,[10] 1 of 1000 phony professors, advocacy spokesperson, etc., actually have authority; in other words, listen to boy actors and teenage feminists for advice. Surely, on examining the typically chaotic and unhappy lives of such media peacocks and mini harridans, they are the very last category of person a child should be listening to.

2. That children should have opinions in the first place about things that they are not able to properly understand.

And that they should be celebrated for taking action on this opinion in whatever way they chose, or think they chose, based on this information; however well understood or not, and that adults should invariably respect this.

Actually, so much of this attempt to inform children of issues is simply unsuccessful, even at face value. And if this was the only intent, one could reasonably claim it fails. Too often, children literally don't know what they are being informed about – even as they watch and listen. Or even what the point is! This is sometimes revealed when asking a simple question, sometimes to comical response in its innocent, total misunderstanding. Properly conditioned to this form of learning, however, many of the more intelligent will be able to repeat parrot fashion the propaganda content and state the accepted shibboleths (or catechism) with a surprising confidence which belies their true level of understanding. Of course, informing children of issues is only part of the intent insofar as it allows control of their opinion. Indeed, imparting a full appreciation of an issue would be an impediment to this goal of control.

3. That certain issues that are presented or implied as settled and correct, e.g., same sex or multi-sex relationships, alternative family structures, feminist perspectives, multiculturalism, pupil activism, are in fact, not so in the adult world.

However, by presenting such opinions as *Newsround* endorses as positive, or consensus, this of course implies disapproval and wrongness to opposition opinions. This emotional leverage is the foundation of brainwashing. The point doesn't have to be driven home for the children to absorb it, for they hear the same thing every day. And unconsciously find such opinions repeated on their home TV and social media, which thusly reinforces the creation of a binary world of right and wrong; activist and progressive verses selfish and bigot. Their opinion good, the others bad! So bad, indeed, that we have to have laws and jail-time for those who hold them. The literally mad, binary thinkers we see endlessly outraged and swarming to destroy those who disagree with them have their origins here – they were children recently!

Parents studying *Newsround* will find such polarising attitudes revealed in the framing of events; for example, regarding refugees, animals under threat, or environmental problems, and while opposing perspectives may be referred to, the subtlest of suggestions is all that is needed to evoke sympathy for the 'correct' opinions and action. Typically, any follow-up discussion with the teacher reinforces this 'correct' opinion, as it is typically also shared by the teacher, here functioning as a brainwasher-in-chief.

By middle primary the children are so pre-programmed that they already know what to think to be correct for any given topic that *Newsround* chooses to present. This is like operant conditioning in action, as if little pigeons pecking at the right coloured button to get a food pellet.[11] One could claim that the kinder, generally globalist, opinion that children usually express reflects their innate disposition rather than engineered consent, however, while there is indeed some truth in this, it is the fact they are being encouraged to do so that matters here. The innate, but not limitless, kindness of children has evolved to be localised and face-to-face in scale. What would otherwise be a spontaneous and age-appropriate expression of concern (if indeed any!) is managed and reinforced to serve an agenda of which the child is unaware. Further, no adult wisdom is brought to bear on such childish optimistic opinions. They are children, after all, and cannot know the eventual consequences of well-intentioned beliefs (or, more properly, statements) when scaled up from the personal to the societal.

By thusly fixing patterns of right and wrong, *Newsround* builds a political and social consensus, and more importantly establishes a mode of considering issues in this binary manner; with the child naturally seeking the right and approved opinion as the point of any issue they are introduced to. This method underlies almost every issue presented by the news, just as they do in the adult world; an issue is presented, it could be anything, minority women in STEM, celebrity opinion on biodiversity, lack of midwifes in Africa, no girls' only skateboard park, etc., which is expected to be accepted as a problem sufficiently serious for it to be a featured news item, without the need to explicitly describe the underlying assumptions; presumably because if it was, it may not then be considered a problem in the first place![12, 13] Then experts say their piece, a sad child may make a statement, and a solution is suggested that the audience is also expected to accept. i.e., typically more funding, more support, more 'conversations', more government intervention.[14] And, as problems are expressed in terms of government responsibility, so in every case by default is the legitimacy of the state extended; i.e., the government should do something to fix the problem. Such empowering of the state as an agent of their agenda has always been the goal of progressive activists, this is required as they are not able to build organic legitimacy for their agenda within the wider society.

The powerful sense of a broken and divided world is transmitted.

Fixing problems in this view inevitably involves state funding, and such funding, although never discussed, is tacitly assumed to be available without consequence. In this respect, then, *Newsround* reflects and reinforces a childish and magical view of the presence of money in life. The end effect of all these assumptions is to build an obligation to government action. In other words, always more government, more politics and more laws.

One contemporary effect of this development is that precocious upper primary-age children come to consider the government's role in like manner to teenagers from a couple of generations ago.[15] As if they are becoming stupidly political even quicker; a particular form of informed citizen and excellence not imagined when the Curriculum for Excellence was created! This situation is of great concern as a potential incubator of the precociousness and intolerance we currently witness in our new world order.

Further to this consideration, we should note that the argument regarding the nature and influence of *Newsround* content is not dependent on seriously misinformed or prejudicial presentations, for usually they are not especially so. Nor on the inappropriateness of the material, for usually they are of at least some interest to children, and indeed may be topics that otherwise may be useful to consider. Nor is this piece a personal attack on the presenters, who are just youth actors; for commonly, news items are presented professionally and in keeping with the target audience. And finally, it is of course not necessarily a bad thing to celebrate a child's achievement, even if it is exaggerated. Our argument in response to the above points is rather to address a consideration of the whole context in which news takes place, and especially its relentless nature which we have been exploring. The net negative effect depends on most news items seeming, and often being, reasonable; success for *Newsround* is measured by the capture of your child's mind, and this is achieved by subtlety and not by blaring loudspeakers, 1984 style. As with all deceit, it works best softly and with a smiling face.

The most effective propaganda is just repetition.
If you take in a constant message,
that message will corrupt you over time.

The *Newsround* content does not, then, have to be screaming lies and dystopic nonsense. It just has to legitimise the wider media life of certain stories and perspectives, and in doing so encourage children to pick up on pre-existing adult responses. As any adult who has tried to give up watching 'just the rubbish' on TV finds out, it is practically impossible to separate the good from the bad. TV is a drug that does not readily admit a simple accommodation to its power. And so, likewise for children, *Newsround* exerts its baleful influence just by being.

The Effect

Our Children Rewired for Endless MSM

I recall as a child not being remotely interested in any adult news from any source. As children we had our own world and our own news whose scope was strictly limited to utility and relevance in that world. This was enough to get on with and our interest in the wider world was allowed to develop at its own pace until such times as adult topics started to matter. As children, we never discussed, nor wanted to, adult media news events. No teacher would even have thought of encouraging such discussion because she would not want children expressing opinions about topics they know nothing about, and thusly also encouraging precociousness; a restraint now seldom exercised. They would also be aware that this would be akin to braining-washing, and thus, far beyond the then curriculum's intention of literacy, numeracy, polite reliability and bladder control.

Our modern school rejects this antique discretion for full disclosure with, basically, adult news content. It is, of course, argued that the overall effect of such news, and *Newsround* in particular, is positive, in that it introduces and reinforces many useful talking points in class. Also, the argument continues, it is necessary for children to be informed of news events, especially in a globalised, fast-paced world where to be 'left out of the information stream is to be left behind' – so the cliché claims. Those that have argued for this position do so almost exclusively in terms of globalist and social justice perspectives; that is to say, their view of the news is functional and connects to serving this agenda. This is convenient from the point of view of this discussion here, as the supporting claims of children 'challenging perceptions', 'being empowered', 'making a difference', 'relate and empathise', etc., are the polar opposite of my argument.

This emphatic distinction between competing arguments facilitates the reader's decisions on this issue, and too on whether to support the national curriculum's ambitions in this respect.

You can't slide all this information, sad news and future world worry onto a child's plate and expect no side effects from their failure to digest it.

One could alternatively argue that a few minutes of news a day in school does not significantly affect children one way or the other, especially when considered against a backdrop of continual news presence in the home TV and smart phone life. I reject this trivialising 'just a little bit more won't do any harm' argument for the same reason that I reject the positive view of TV news for children; anything that lengthens exposure and strengthens false legitimacy increases harm in proportion. Leverage has always relied on 'it's only a little bit' and 'what's the harm' to gradually increase its power. As we know by personal example, media news has infiltrated our domestic routines to the extent that many adults are in thrall to the tune of hours every day; even so, few of these same adults think that this is a good thing. The globalised world has surely demonstrated to us that there are human limits to our capacity to process disparate information.

TV news; drinking information from a hosepipe.

In the development of our argument against our children watching news in school we introduce a caveat; although the effects I discuss do have a simple cause, their operation is not simple or direct. We need to consider cause and effect operating through several orders of iteration. The early and relentless exposure to the nonsense, trauma and precocious opinion that comprises the news will take years to find its strongest expression in the confused, stressed and distracted adult, but nevertheless on this journey continues to do mental and spiritual harm. Already we note the stirrings of this in primary school among the more sensitive children, although the proper linkage between this sad development and exposure to toxic media junk and relentless TV news has not been fully explored. I note, though, that a recent reference to the effect of such media garbage on children's mental welfare was ironically (triumphantly?) mentioned on Google news itself; at once, creator and messenger of its own bad news! Thus do the global Beast companies mock us to our very faces!

BBC *Newsround*: The Rectangle of Lies

> Exchange connection for hyper connection
> of a life literally lived in another realm
> as human material for digital processing
> the drug addiction to the screen,
> surreal jump-cuts, emotions feminised
> the validation of the pop world
> the fawning over attention whores
> poptarts showboating compassion
> and socially destructive delusions
> presented as truth to gullible young
> to turn them from themselves.

One has to consider this argument, then, as an ensemble years in the assembling and imagine the manufacture of new opinions as a multi-layered, multi-generational project, a sort of 'combined assault', with *Newsround* as just one element of the attack.[16]

Another important consideration when examining the effect of *Newsround* is the fact that children do not make the same connections between cause and effect as an adult. We have already noted how children can misunderstand to the extent of the exact opposite; properly considered, this is a source of comically instructed wisdom for the teacher. Such a thing, of course, never occurred with the traditional 3R curriculum. However, setting the humorous aside, this consideration is of extreme importance when introducing ideas that have a societal significance and contain a psychological impact. Backstories are seldom explained and a child may be incapable of understanding context, but what they will pick up on, however, is the emotional content and the functional intent of the information. They understand how they are expected to respond to a news item in a way that would elicit adult approval. This is the start point of brainwashing. The victim wants to agree.

And the most obvious effect of this is that *Newsround* in particular, but all TV news by extension, is legitimised as a proper source of information regarding the world. Even more importantly, its world view is tacitly endorsed along with the values and the life choices and tech gadgetry it propagates. Endorsed by further extension, although completely invisible and unknowable to the children, is the world plan of the four horsemen of the apocalypse currently disguised as tech giants-Google, Amazon, Facebook and Apple; your friendly neighbourhood mega-corporations who collaborate to create, control, and manipulate information, messaging and visual imagery. Also included among the endorsements are other media conglomerates, the outriders of the death's head four, their related advertising agencies and show business interests. And finally, by further extension and implication, the whole enabling (and disabling) world of smart phones, social media, new apps and computer life. All this obtained just by watching. Our children have no chance against this crushing ever present psychosis of flashing, coloured images. It is not unreasonable to conclude that our overlords will not be content until every asset on Earth is digitalised and controlled under their all-seeing eye; this to soon include assigning a digital identity to our children. As if cattle, or perhaps better termed, goyim.

Their future vision: digital control of everything.

Children become habituated to this form of dissemination of knowledge and opinions; today's top story, regular updates, the 'expert' opinion, so-called surveys which mould, not express, opinion. They are surely encouraged to become addicted to pop fluff and media trivia, idol worship, clickbait and product placement, and then find the whole reinforced in the adult world of their parents. They find the issues that they 'should' be concerned about (racism, multiculturalism, human and sex rights, the environment, equality, cuddly animals), are given the terms and concern templates, and exposed to proper expression of these via child friendly actresses or apparently amazing, but actually manufactured, child activists – the recent Greta T being a spectacular example of the latter. The watching child is not aware that many topics covered are not value neutral or settled issues in the real world and that a mild expression of a contrary view by the presenter does not necessarily by itself constitute a balanced position in what may be a complicated topic sporting a range of opinions.

The issue at hand here is not so much a question of facts, as one of attitude and intent. Considered politically, this situation is far more capable of controlling dissent than any state (or any other interest) could by any other means, including direct repression. Considered ideologically, *Newsround* could be regarded as a programme to subtly facilitate the transmission of new cultural norms, and, as such, a form of psychological warfare. Lest this seem an overstatement, we note that the great societal madness that has descended upon us all depends for its success on finding us willing to accept its tenets; *Newsround* is that first, subtle preparation. To achieve this objective it need not directly attack traditional society. Merely ignoring the natural bonds and features of community, or subtly repackaging them as celebrations of something else instead, helps quietly make them disappear. Having weakened thusly their traditional world of reference, the child is opened to alternatives – *Newsround* has already done its job!

Those who control the message, control the receiver; this is why they want news in school.

The parent may hope that the class teacher would provide a mature overview in such a situation, however, as she consumes the same news and typically only understands the same biases, this hope would be a forlorn one. Indeed, many teachers are not only activists for the progressive viewpoints expressed on *Newsround*, they would consider such proselytising as a proper thing to do and, indeed, are so empowered by the curriculum under the four Talmudic outcomes; global citizen, mini golem, trainee harridan and justice bot. It is not hard to find teachers boastfully proud of their role in this regard. However, we should not think of this teacher influence after the manner of a party commissar berating pupils for lack of Marxist-Leninist zeal in exposing counter-revolutionary parents, for such influence is at its most powerful when gentlest, even unwitting. The smallest gesture of assent carries the day in this battle.

Endorsing certain viewpoints and interests, necessarily means not endorsing others. Thusly, certain topics or perspectives are silently delegitimised merely by their exclusion; for example, positive portrayals of ethnic Whites, historical events which do not include the multicultural community and uplifting European cultural identity. Indeed, anything which confronts the deception of the multicultural and sexual agenda. Of particular existential concern here to native White welfare is the delegitimisation of the family, and especially motherhood; this done by means of the modern consensus, and BBC approved, life purpose for little girls – that being, the strong women with independent careers. This is presented, in this age of collapsing White birth rates, with more enthusiasm than survival warrants.

This 'strong woman' trope powerfully transmitted by *Newsround* is not yet directly repackaged as blows against the patriarchy – this will come in a few years as the girls enter puberty – but the idea is always present in referencing female achievements. This focus on rebel girls doing men stuff, smashing ceilings and tackling gender grievances, gives false and self-defeating goals to little girls and prevents them celebrating themselves as girls with girl ambitions, and especially the greatest one – that of motherhood. Although such views are aimed at the girl audience, the wider psychological and societal impacts damage all sexes, although principally the main two. Essentially, this is a form of emotional abuse. It is a testimony to the travesty of our education system that few teachers could even countenance the idea that such apparent pro-fem remarks could ever have a negative effect, far less a catastrophic one.

Mental health issues must start somewhere; how about here!

If we consider that our children's psyches are pummelled day after day with stressful and deceitful narratives, sudden jump-cuts between disparate topics, and the relentless imagery of the multimedia, we are led to reflect on the fact that such unprotected exposure produces fatigue, confusion and fear. Although experienced in a classroom, psychologically such exposure mimics the stress of being unprotected in an unfamiliar place. We have seen many recent examples, in the presidency of Trump and our Brexit process, of such media-driven responses feeding a literal derangement among adults; the same operates on children. In our emotional regulation much depends on the stability and predictability of our social environment, who can doubt, then, that TV news is a negative contributor to that environment. That *Newsround* itself is less than ten minutes long may lead one to forget the fact that its destabilising effect does not suddenly stop with the end of the programme; for, directly referenced by the teacher or spread as feedback from classmates, it reverberates in the mind. And then the same the next day:

Homeless children sleeping rough on Britain's streets.

and

> *We look at the children in care while their parents struggled with addiction or violence issues.*

That *Newsround* 'balances' its coverage of tragedy and crisis with chirpy upbeat tales and fluffy media trash only serves to confirm the negative psychic power of the former. This 'cheerful' nonsense news provides a polarising background to the bad news which, rather than ameliorating it, ironically serves to emphasise it by the contrast. The effect on mental health of so much information, unprocessed and continually piled atop the previous day's ration, may take years to fully manifest, but it will. A commonly suggested solution to this enervation is to 'declutter' by deleting news apps and avoid TV news. But how much better for your children not to start on this path of news stress and avoid it in the first place by deleting *Newsround*?

Newsround, the first step in the 'Men are Pigs' project

A final aspect of our argument that is of especial relevance to boys' well-being is how feminine *Newsround* presentation is, both in style and content. Of course, it intends to be gender neutral, but the editorial choices reveal the essentially female outlook and direction. All the fluff media features (*Bake Off, Britain's Got Talent, Brit Awards*, etc.), celebrity updates, charity initiatives, animal welfare and pop news, appeal overwhelmingly to a female, or female-minded, audience. Likewise, the assumption (or encouragement with helpline numbers) of 'sensitivity', and the invitation to comment on the website (aka, female herd agreement!), is just like the big girl's world of social media. The 'boys' topics that do feature, team sports for example, should have no place in school as TV viewing; really, do boys need more exposure to TV football and sports celebrities as role models? Although the team sports features appeal more to boys, it would be a mistake to consider this inclusion as a concession to their interests, for such boy-friendly features are weaponised in keeping with the *Newsround* agenda. And so, they are presented in such a way as to make it clear to the viewers that the topic is to be considered as gender neutral. The children know instinctively that it is not; thus cognitive dissonance is introduced into their lives, and they become a little more uncentred from what is understood, without words, as true. By implying that girls are more interested, in football, for example, than they really are (and really, honestly, they usually aren't[17]) this suggests to them that they should be; thereby manipulating their innate sense of girls' interests and wider attitudes.

For the boys, this is a silent reminder that they have no exclusive places or interests, and that where these are found they must be shared and/or surrendered, not as a concession, but as a Female Right. If females want access to what is, by preference and tradition, male, then this must be surrendered regardless, and *Newsround* will celebrate this. This is the start of the removal of private male space from public life, a development that has seen its apogee in successful aggressive lawfare against boys and male organisations to the eventual detriment of everyone.

This phenomenon has recently redounded to girls' private spaces (e.g., Girl Guides) with the same intent and the same eventual effect. In its illustration of this aspect of the sex war, *Newsround* plays a full role in presenting boys and girls as potential enemies over our shared culture.

It is not our intention here to discuss the war against boys, but, in a primary school world that is already overwhelmingly and presumptuously feminine, we consider *Newsround* as the axis propaganda department. Too often, topics presented carry the implication of negative societal male power; for example, the proportion of ethnic-others in STEM, or the operation of the 'glass ceiling' on women executives. Even when considering an aspect of exclusive relevance to boys, it presents a negative slant with boys unwittingly representing something to be opposed or changed. For example, presenting clichéd straw men (straw boys?) addressing phony boy problems, like the need for boys to get in touch with their feelings more (to be more like girls, presumably), or celebrating traditional boys interests when they are colonised by girls (e.g., *The girls who are showing that they can be just as good as boys at xxx*); *Newsround*, then, adds to the overall femininity of school life and the male-negative societal message as boys receive and understand it. One wonders if some of the faggotisation one witnesses among younger men has, in addition to the environmental chemical attack on their testosterone levels, a sort of half-conscious acclimatisation (or emulation) to this feminised speeched and gestured world depicted daily on screen?

The media that our boys consume feminises them as it demonises.

When all is girly, this contains an implicit message about boys' proper place in the future world; their attributes and interests are by default negative. As if it was an assignment, hopelessness settles on boyish endeavours. This message buried deep in the limbic memory to find its inevitable effect in the following decades, but all the while reinforced by our entire Western media, especially with respect to White males. Our boys will grow up with this sense of something being not quite right about themselves, perhaps even coming to believe that they are members of that privileged group that is the source of everyone else's problem, the evil White patriarchy. And thus deserving of their doom which they can easily hear celebrated across the mainstream media, although not yet by *Newsround*.

It's a girl's world now: The 'All Men are Pigs' project intended to split the sexes, and make (White) men the target of societal hatred, censure, and distrust, is firmly established in our culture and legal system. And James Brown' song is now a supreme example of sexism and irony, and the big wheel of history turning.[18]

BBC *Newsround*: whoever owns the children's minds wins the country.

Where is the righteous hate for this globalist propaganda, preaching tolerance and diversity instead of discipline and respect? Plugging our children into the spirit-death machine of popworld garbage as they sit defenceless in the classroom, unaware that BBC *Newsround* is the mass graveyard of their culture. The exact opposite of being informed; our children deformed by this enemy force placed inside their heads, filing them with trivia, endorsements and agitprop worry. Consider the brain rewiring effect of this relentless assault; the child's mind either floats in this psychedelic terrain, or is jarred from one topic to another. Too much reality, but not a lot of truth! It does not matter to those behind this whether children understand what they watch, or care, for they will still absorb the agenda. *Newsround* is like a gateway drug to further programming, making news junkies and future clients, and not incidentally, creating a next generation of depressed, unhappy and confused kids for the next generation of drug therapies and apps to lock them further into digital enslavement. Your kids; BBC *Newsround* hates them.

The devil usually wears a smiling face, but right now he's laughing.

What To Do?

The ten minutes of *Newsround* could be so much better spent by doing anything else as long as it didn't involve a screen. How about listening to a piece of classical music, looking at a piece of art, analysing a poem or, if a proper understanding of the world is desired for the children, read the Bible or the Greek myths.

How about just sit quietly while *Newsround* is NOT on. And think whatever you want!

5
The Holocaust

Your Fate Has Been Decided. Resistance Is Futile

Achtung, Achtung! Report at once for Holocaust training.

It is the intention here to explore principles and issues raised by the study of the Holocaust in primary schools and specifically the effect of such study on our children. The Holocaust is already studied as a, often *the*, major component in the study of the Second World War. Its presence in schools is greater than this, however, having its own week of remembrance, numerous stories issued as class reading and regularly evoked, often by reference to Anne Frank, in general exhortations regarding tolerance and racism. This is apparently not enough and, in response, there has been a global Jewish effort to officially incorporate a kosher approved study of the Holocaust into the Western nations' national curricula. This has been largely successful, as its advocates and co-ethnic owned media have been able to claim that Western nations are rife with racial and anti-Jewish hatreds. This is a straight lie and a calumny on us. Nevertheless, we are getting more Holocaust in primary schools – and this will be 'celebrated'. Here I mostly refer to Scotland, as this is my area of expertise and special concern, but this argument is valid for all the UK and probably all the Western world.

We know the story of the Holocaust, or think we do, and we understand the intended message as stated, but what other messages underlie this vast, internationally coordinated tale of woe flown under the Magen David? Except where it connects to our stated intention, I wish to avoid discussing this topic. Likewise, this is not a discussion of the character and history of the Jews; such references as occur are warranted by the subject of this study:

But here I feel empowered by the nature of my obligation to our children to note, without fear, outsized Jewish power and its role in the creation of the dysfunction in we see in Western nations and the presence, if not role, of the Holocaust in this process.

I will not state all the caveats and denials normally attendant upon a discussion of this topic, you may imagine them, and more, as a given – although we know that this justification will avail us little protection against the inevitable accusations. This, then, is the ethical and emotional pupil backdrop to the study of the Holocaust.

My argument here is a simple one, and stands valid irrespective of one's attitude to the Holocaust as a specific topic within, or without, the study of the Second World War: There are negative consequences for the mental and spiritual well-being of primary-age children in studying this horror topic.[1] In order to make this this evident we must deconstruct and then assemble. Bear with me.

Background

The importance of this topic needs no defence, as the modern world's politics is predicated on it. On a daily basis articles about the Holocaust are syndicated through MSM news and turning on your TV at any time would probably allow you to find a programme or report on the subject. Even, when properly considered, much of Western entertainment culture, both content and values, has a direct line connection too; the obsession with the Second World War, endless references to Hitler, movie exhortations to tolerance, cardboard cut-out Nazis in TV drama, the clear Zionist motivation behind many Hollywood produced plots. In our daily life, especially as presented in the media, claims regarding racism, intolerance and anti-Semitism hover, a judge's gavel righteously poised, above certain topics, and enforced hate speech laws, to name but one form of ruin waiting for the careless phrase or presumed opinion, can all be traced back to what happened to the Jews.

Hitler is everywhere now in endless multiples. You don't even have to be called Adolf, anyone can be a Hitler for any reason. Or none.

This is a topic for other scholars and we note it to reference its undeniable power, which in contrast to the usual course of memory, is increasing as the time distance from the origin increases – the consensus opinion regarding the Holocaust not being subject to the usual revisionism that accompanies every other historical topic after a similar time period. The war itself has been subject to much revisionism, and although not all of it has yet reached public consciousness (i.e., *The History Channel*), it is now accepted that the story is more complex and morally ambivalent than was formerly realised, or could have been accepted, and one can now find blame and infamy, subterfuge and hidden interests shifted to unexpected locations on the checkerboard of history. Except for the Holocaust![2] It seems to stand outside of history, immutable, as if a religion. And this point leads us to the most striking aspect of the Holocaust; that of the increasing use of fully enforced, legal sanction against revisionists, as if against religious apostates. Excepting the personal and professional ruin accompanying an 'outing' as an anti-Semite, for which accusation there is no defence – regardless of the falsity of the allegation – our own country has avoided this singular refashioning of blasphemy laws, but pressure is increasing for us to fall in line with many other Western nations and jail revisionist scholars, or unfortunately curious members of the public, as hateful deniers, anti-Semites and even worse, celebrants of the final solution. Probably in this regard we in the UK will fall in line with Jewish demands, via EU or UN proxies, in the near future. We note in illustration of this point the recent vigorous advocacy on behalf of his ethnic group (and frankly astonishing lese-majesty) by government minister Robert Jenrick in calling for the punishment of those who show insufficient deference to the Jewish world view: 'I will use my position as Secretary of State to write to all universities and local authorities to insist that they adopt the IHRA [International Holocaust Remembrance Alliance] definition [of anti-Semitism] at the earliest opportunity…and use it when considering matters such as disciplinary procedures. Failure to act in this regard is unacceptable.'

It is astonishing that a non-native ethnic group can make it illegal to discuss fundamental aspects of their and our collective history.

The message could not be clearer: an exclusive group with exclusive interests makes its pitch to control the public dialogue and make you embrace their punishing experiences; thusly placing itself beyond moral scrutiny. And so, Holocaust revisionists MUST BE PUNISHED.

The Holocaust has, then, become a pseudo-religion of persecution within a religion already obsessed with victimhood. It has been argued that this sensibility, reinforced by their tragic history, partly explains why the Jews, as a people, are particularly intolerant of criticism and have used their powerful levers of patronage within the political and legal systems to push for anti-Semitic laws and various curtailments of free speech. The Holocaust has undoubtedly enabled this. Invoking it and claims of anti-Semitism to silence criticism of Israeli action or untoward Jewish influence – and, of course, unwanted discussion of the Holocaust.[3] Paraphrasing Inigo Montoya: *You keep using that word. It does not mean what you think it means.*

This same obsession may also explain the truly staggering number of official and unofficial Jewish advocacy and intel organisations policing the world for so-called anti-Semites – and routinely manufacturing the same as false flag deceptions to justify claims of still continuing prejudice. This furnace of paranoia stoked even in Scotland; a recently exposed online anti-Semite in actuality another Zionist false flag operation. Jews playing both sides to better control the public mind. In light of this it is not unreasonable to consider whether this obsessive in-group focus has seriously distorted their collective moral compass and wonder about the consequences of this on Gentile host populations.

There can be no doubt, then, that the study of the Holocaust in our primary schools forever lowers us into this world of distrust and paranoia. For us, Nazi is embedded in our lexicon and, one way or another, we will be involved in the Greater Israel project. Notwithstanding the claims that universal lessons are to be learned, others will come to see the special pleading for what it is, and become resentful.[4] Eventually, this will lead (as it has elsewhere in the West) to divisive accusations, punishments and the creation of new, but Gentile, victims. It is astonishing that Jewish Holocaust education advocates do not see a future danger in this course.

Plus ça change, plus c'est la même chose.

Our Duty as Parents and Teachers

It is our duty as parents and teachers to protect our children from ideas and situations that are inappropriate lest we confuse or corrupt them. We do this of course because their level of development is such that they cannot intellectually understand, nor emotionally process, these topics as adults can.

Many parents realise that our children face well-funded and aggressively advanced attempts to normalise in childhood many adult categories of consideration like sexuality, human rights, and political activism.

Some argue in contrast to this, however, that children should be exposed to the world as it is, and that this should be done as soon as possible. Reasoning that, as the world already relentlessly presses upon our children's sensibilities through TV and their personal devices, we would be as well managing this as best we can. Rather than denying it and attempting, as young Buddha's father tried to do, to shield them from the world's turmoil – which in the end only postpones the inevitable confrontation and increases the pain of adjustment. At this point, we hardly need to be reminded that many topics, formerly absent from childhood consideration as deemed of adult concern, are now frequent visitors to the classroom. This pro-realworld position envisages the parent or teacher sitting down and discussing the worries and confusions of certain topics or encouraging them to click on the links for online support! If this is done sensitively and with proper concern for balance, they argue, it helps promote all the qualities of understanding and concern that we wish to encourage in the future citizens that our pupils and children will become.

This seems, at face value, a valid argument, but then begs some practical questions regarding proper content, appropriate sensitivity and political balance; who decides, who presents, and how well do they (if they do, or even if they can) present such material.[5] Which particular topics are children to be shielded from, or conversely, which are promoted and discussed? Or is every single topic in our depressed and broken world to be up for discussion with children, regardless? Considering this, we must surely wonder whether topics that come pre-loaded with care and complexity, and perhaps controversy, are handled to best satisfaction in the classroom. In my opinion they cannot be.

They cannot be for three reasons, namely; the limitations inherent in the material itself, those of the presenter and those of the pupils. Let us examine them in turn.

The first limitation is that some issues are fundamentally not reducible to a neutral position, as they are expressly predicated on a politicised view of things. This is especially true of issues involving social justice, whether current or historical. In addition, such issues seldom permit even a settled difference of opinion, instead leaving in their wake everything unresolved – except entrenched opinions, which are further strengthened! We have seen countless recent examples of this phenomenon in action with respect to, for example, climate or sexuality; as a society, we seem to be increasingly losing the ability to find a middle ground, or accept others' viewpoints and move on.

Turning to the Holocaust, and the Second World War in general, this most definitely falls into this first limitation, for no view can be permitted, but the established one. Further, there is no age-appropriate adjustment possible which could introduce nuance – it's slogans all the way down! And German guilt must be absolutely fixed, notwithstanding the possibility of a reference to some injustices against Germany in the Versailles Treaty of the First World War; the which, at the level of explanation offered, cannot be properly appreciated by listening children.

The second limitation with contentious material is the expertise and sensitivity of the presenter of such material, in our case, the primary school teacher. There is no intention on my part to especially denigrate the overwhelmingly female presenters, but merely to note that, with reference to the Holocaust as a feature of the war, by knowledge and interest they are generally not adequate to the task; commonplace knowledge of the war and the culture of the first half of the 20th century is no longer to be assumed, and doubly so if of a non-native ethnicity. Examples of this ignorance are easy to find on viewing the display material of a class studying the Second World War.[6]

The third limitation we will return to later in detail; here we make a general point that, given that children, even of the same age, differ in their level of emotional maturity and intellectual ability to appreciate the moral or political message inherent in certain topics, we should be concerned that their take-away message may not be what we think it should be? Of course, children might parrot the correct opinion, but other deeper currents have been set in motion. Indeed, we have already noted children repeating the consensus opinion about a topic and thusly apparently demonstrating successful social engineering – but without them knowing what they meant by their words, and even completely misunderstanding the intended message to the extent of reversing it.

We ask, then, when complex or contentious issues are introduced; are children properly informed, or even, can they be? Do they fairly understand the material presented, or are they being propagandised? Do they come to care about the issues of their own volition, or can such force feeding actually bring about the opposite? With respect to the Holocaust, are children properly sensitised by the content, over-sensitised or perhaps, in contrast, desensitised? Or, as is more likely, all of these things simultaneously, varying from pupil to pupil? No one has an answer to these questions; we are just supposed to accept, as an article of faith, that illustrating injustice leads the young mind to embrace justice. However, we contend that the end effect of all this presentation and discussion of the world's problems, under the auspices of justice, is more likely to overload our children with cares and misunderstandings before their time? Further, it is not a good argument to defend the teaching of the Holocaust by claiming that children are exposed to distressing stories anyway; for it is just such stories that are the foundations of the future stress that we should be protecting our children from. Is this situation not a bit like an adult watching TV news at breakfast and always leaving for work either depressed or furious?

The experts behind these policy initiatives are not experts at all, they are political operators on the public purse.

This concern for the proper understanding of a complex and terrible topic, and its longer term impact on sensibility and well-being, is a general one relevant to anyone who cares about children and our society's future. And it extends beyond the Holocaust. Nor is this argument assuming fragility on the part of children. I note that children often are practical and robust in response to disturbing knowledge, and that this quality is to be encouraged where it is necessary, although not solicitously striven for. However, innocence deserves some freedom before it is lost; and until the right time for such loss, we recognise that a topic can be fundamentally inappropriate in its content and its implications for immature minds. A topic like the Holocaust.

The Argument for Teaching the Holocaust

It would be nice to think that our children's idea of wicked first comes in the pantomime form of a witch or an angry ogre in a fairy tale. Certainly such tales can be surprisingly cruel, however, they are properly located in fantasy land, scaled right and pitched to level for a child to build on a developing real world sensibility. If death occurs in such tales it is containable in the child's mind by being justified and simply presented in a fantasy context. Not so with the Holocaust.

We would surely expect that primary-age children have never before considered such an idea as the extermination of an entire population and that this would turn up as inexplicable and a shock, even allowing for the increased exposure of our children to the world's ugliness and confusion.[7]

An argument can be made for converting this shock into impetus for good. Good here meaning future social justice. Our children are, after all, exhorted by their curriculum to be thus concerned; why not then, make fast this same ambition by nailing to our mast the Holocaust as a banner, signalling the seriousness of our intent by beginning our voyage to future global social justice by referencing the great insult to this in our modern age. If this is upsetting, it would be argued – then good! That's its job. Any gainsayers could be responded to by claiming that the Holocaust is the final destination on this road to bigotry; this is where you eventually end up when you have no understanding of the other, no tolerance of difference. Hate and blame and persecution, fired up by demagogues, creep into the public discourse. Let's nip this ugly flower of intolerance in the bud by fearlessly telling its story.

A Holocaust museum in every class.

As *the* real-life example of intolerance of others intentionally manipulated to irrational hatred, nothing beats the Holocaust as the default topic.[8] There is no doubt of its dramatic interest for children; the highly personalised nature of the tragedy, typically focused on child victims for better identification (and previously read as class-issued novels), and the morbid details which fascinate children, can be balanced out somewhat – only somewhat, by necessity of the message's intent – with uplifting endings, as required. Later, in high school, children can complete their Holocaust education by a school pilgrimage to Auschwitz.

1. What Is the Message of the Holocaust?

The stated intent is that our pupils come away with a unique understanding of the ultimate end of intolerance and persecution, but specifically (because this is what the Holocaust actually is, as opposed to 'just' a regular genocide) the special persecution of Jews.[9]

But what happens to this notion of genocide, this intreasured seed of intended evil and implied guilt, once it is planted in the virgin soil of the unploughed Gentile mind?

Does it, as assumed, stimulate in the schoolchild an informed awareness of intolerance in action and a concomitant compassion for racial justice? There is no evidence for this; for pity and compassion are natural attributes that are not to be made to a formula. It is the inner compass that directs the soul towards justice, and trying to bend the needle against this force often results in something getting twisted. Whatever this 'something' is becomes particularly apposite when it involves the telling of a tragic epic as a vehicle for a particular moral and political message. And moreover, one that involves compromising the present with hate laws. There are many conclusions that could be derived from a study of the Holocaust, forcing children to adopt just one smacks of the very propaganda that the Holocaust story stands in opposition to.

Even the basic principle, and apparent great truth, that is claimed to underlie the Holocaust message, that hate is born of ignorance and that this eventually leads to persecution, is a proposition that is not examined. This is because it is not true; hate (however defined) need not come from ignorance or intolerance, nor be irrational and lead to persecution. Furthermore, this is a message that is generally not applicable to modern European peoples. Many recent, and still continuing, tragic events throughout Europe involving the criminal persecution and murder of native Europeans by immigrant ethnic-others have not resulted in any backlash against the perpetrator's community, could be cited as proof of the unusually open-minded and law-abiding nature of Europeans.

Of course, in arguing for learning lessons from history to build tolerance and encourage compassion, one finds that this message runs up hard against the Israeli 700km wall enclosing the Palestinian world into a not-compassionate concentration camp.[10] And also the not so tolerant, and ever increasing in scope, legislation censuring any criticism, or even queries, regarding Jews, whether historical or contemporary. This is like a Jewish version of:

You dare to question the authority of a Gestapo colonel;
...silence schweinhund!

Likewise, passing reference may be made to other genocides in world history, although not any that could reflect badly on direct Jewish involvement; for example, the claimed and celebrated exterminations of the Hittites, Amorites, Girgashites, Amalekites,

Perizzites, Canaanites, Midianites, Jebusites and Edomites, as described in the Old Testament. Or, at the other end of the time spectrum, serving the Bolshevik Moloch in the Russian Revolution. Also skipped out of the narrative is any explanation of why the Holocaust happened with respect to possible (or more rather, even the slightest possibility of) Jewish culpability.[11] We recall here the impossibility of discussing this, and that anti-Semitism claims are noted as the fastest travelling denouncements, with a whole secret army devoted to searching them out, minute by minute. You don't even have to deny the Holocaust to be accused of Holocaust denial, and ruined just the same. Just writing this has done so for me.

2. What Is the Unstated Message of the Holocaust?

We cannot doubt that there is an ethical and historical message from the Holocaust to us, even us in Scotland with the scarcest of connections to it, and that the promulgation of this message is an intention of the Holocaust initiatives – this much is obvious. The exhortation to future moral goodness consequent on this message is also obvious. But what about the message not stated; what is that?

To answer, we ask: when they study the Holocaust, what are our children to make of the images of marching, uniformed, swastika'd youth, banging drums; or pretty mädchen, also swastika'd, doing gymnastics, and their relationship to persecution and murder? The answer leads to a conclusion of German racial psychopathy. Here the entire German nation, in the Nazi era and still in our own time, is forever impugned; the sins of the fathers visited, as per Old Testament admonitions, on the sons. This suggestion of something untoward about the Germans, a national trait of efficient, bureaucratic cruelty, a psychology of sociopathy seguing to psychopathy, is a powerful one with a false pedigree going back to the First World War. Further, this suggestion of a nation of psychopaths exists independently of knowledge of the concept itself:

How could it be otherwise, when we see the same repeated images of vast rallies and cheering, ordinary Germans ecstatic at hearing their apoplectic führer, tacitly attesting to this apparent guilt of all Germans as anti-Semites, and worse! – Hitler's willing executioners, to reference a well-received book covering this topic.[12]

This is the source of the painfully apparent, contemporary German guilt, but travelling alongside is supposed Gentile complicity. This expressed as indifference to Jewish suffering and, more directly, deliberate failure to act to prevent or lessen it, in itself an expression of the same deeply rooted, anti-Semitism – although obviously muted in comparison to the Germans. As the direct link to the Holocaust is soon to disappear, Gentiles are being increasingly, and increasingly vociferously, reminded of this particular spin to the story. It is likely that this shift in focus will become, as it has in the USA, the essence of the 21stCentury Holocaust message, and thusly that transmitted to our children in school. This need is what lies behind the massive lobbying in the USA to have the 'Never Again' Holocaust Education Act passed making the Holocaust integral to the curriculum.

In the Holocaust narrative, the sins of the Nazis fall on all Germans. And on all Gentiles by association.

Thus, although the perfidy may fall on the Germans, it radiates degrees of complicity to other Gentiles; French, Ukrainians and Polish top the list, but it eventually includes us here in Scotland. This is the tacit message to us and our children; you shall not get off scot free of blame. Any European White person can turn into an anti-Semite for apparently no reason at all, except irrational prejudice. Some Jewish commentators have claimed that such anti-Semitism is foundational to Gentile European culture and indeed inherent in our Euro DNA.[13] Thus explaining this recurrent Jewish persecution we see throughout European history starting with the Romans.

It is not a trivial thing to imply that ethnic Whites chronically lack tolerance to different others or even harbour hidden hatreds, when the opposite is evidently the case. As a characteristic of our innate ethics mated to Christian moral universalism, no society has been as open or generous to suppliant outsiders than ours. The justice and racial tolerance, referred to as the goal of Holocaust training, we have already achieved. Yet no 'celebration' of this is ever acknowledged. The constant reinforcement of this anti-bigotry message is not needed *for us*, but aimed *at us* as a weapon to shame, and thereby demoralise and lay open to manipulation. Our extreme empathy and moral reasoning, our obvious need for a moral reputation to self and others, has been recognised and exploited, and then flipped to become maladaptive to our well-being. Such well-learned guilt reinforces the self-hating indoctrination of the other six of the harmful seven.

We are a people with amnesia, encouraged to forget our historical decency which still lives within us.

Thus does the Holocaust turn a jaundiced eye on ourselves; or more properly, this darkly tinted view of ourselves is passed to our children. This dark view is false, but more importantly, it is culturally lethal to view our nation's history as a catalogue of exploitation, deceit and betrayal.[14] Following on from this, it is not chauvinist to say that we have much to be proud of, and that this must be known and strongly founded in children before they are in a position to hear and understand criticism of it, so that they do not come to hate their own land before they know it.[15] And that ethnic newcomers, with no claim on this pride, do not come to hate Scotland before they too know it.

This implied message, then, can be considered as yet another add-on to the psy-ops package that is our children's education.[16]

3. What Is the Hidden Message of the Holocaust?

In considering the exclusively negative message to Gentile Europeans within the Holocaust's universalist message, another message suggests itself as a kind of opposite: a special plead for Jews within the gigantic catastrophe of the war – because this is what actually happens in the focus on the Holocaust. Other non-Jewish victims will be referenced, as required by expediency within a debate, but they don't matter for the Holocaust narrative, not really; no one tells their story, or makes movies about their suffering or their eventual triumph. And the most brutal evidence for this lack of concern is the lack of reparations for the others.

But reparations depends on guilt, and guilt has to be continually topped-up as it naturally lessens. And so we find, following Professor Finkelstein's[17] argument, that as genocide was industrialised, so too has the Holocaust as an historical event itself become industrialised. Jewish impresarial skills, banking leverage and political connections have combined to create a chimera blending political advantage, entertainment, employment and reparations whose scope is the whole Western world. This is an industry whose hidden goal is to exploit grief to blindside others and stymie criticism of Jewish self-aggrandisement, and particularly their high level control of the public mind. And to intimidate critics of Israeli realpolitik in the Middle East and the open wound of the Palestinians. Ultimately, it aims to de-legitimise the normal historical revisionist process as a threat to the entire edifice of special victimisation with its attached financial reparations. In short, to bend us to their will and shekel farm us – hence, goyim. This intention is not without implications for our own children.

Of course, while turning a critical eye on Gentile past and present, there is one country to whom we may not direct this Holocaust-inspired concern for tolerance, lest such an observation mocks the message it proclaims. Informed adults notice this and sometime wonder if the lesson of the Holocaust has been reversed to become a template.[18] This goes beyond simple hypocrisy, though, for at this point we enter into the realm of evolutionary group psychology. Here victimhood experiences have far-reaching, and possibly endless, negative consequences for the relations between groups. And, as referred to in the anti-bullying chapter, such feelings stimulate the need for revenge, which in a multi-ethnic country, and in the context of competition over resources, can have only one eventual outcome. History repeatedly demonstrates this for us.

We can see daily in other countries of the world the most appalling persecutions without a cheep from politicians and the mainstream media and Twitter mobs, and wonder rhetorically why that is so. And wonder too, what has happened to the universalist message of the Holocaust, and how we should factor this apparent anomaly into our school Holocaust training? But know also the personal danger that stepping outside of a strict adherence to the Holocaust orthodoxy would bring.[19] For this reason and for everything that is not, and cannot be, said, the Holocaust and its message should be a topic to steer clear of.

The big message is, don't mess with the Jews.

And Our Children in Scotland?

While singular in its scale, the Holocaust as a story of ruin and death, is just one more insult added to the developing sensibility and world view of our children. Finding themselves in the centre of a story full of tragedy which they improperly understand and which tarnishes the shine due to ancestors, while transferring guilt to themselves, we wonder what happens to this unprocessed disquiet?

Here we need to consider the egocentric nature of a child and how information, of developmental necessity, gets processed with reference to themselves; the child thinks: How does this connect with me? The spoken answer is vouchsafed, but the unanswerable aspects, the confusion and the guilt, is internalised to sit and fester.

Parents look to your own, there is no one in the educational establishment to protect them from psychological assault and propaganda.

It is my argument, then, that the direct effect of this is psychologically negative. And that studying the Holocaust does not encourage concern, love or compassion for others. And, should higher order thinking eventually lead you here, you will come to realise that the Holocaust lessons were not so much about the past, as a distraction while the future was planned – a future with implanted guilt disguised as morality. In this scenario, we become a threat to ourselves, years of shame stretc.h out ahead; this then, is an aspect of the Great Madness that seems to have culturally overwhelmed us.

One wonders if, in that nether region of the collective hostile mind, where hatred shows its true face and inspires, by circuitous self-deceiving and hidden routes, the wicked levers that control the world, this confusion and self-hatred was not all along an actual intention; plant the lack of respect, deny the ability to query the same by the law, and with complicit on-board educational experts and useful idiot-teachers, just leave the desired result to time.[20]

Those whom the Elders would rule unhindered, they first make mad.

Lest this seem too fanciful, too vasty in scope, consider as evidence one's own knowledge of how such a resentfully motivated enemy, say in an employment situation, can pursue the unjust ruin of another, often by secret means and over much time and space. And at the other end of the scale spectrum, the Holocaust itself; is this indeed, not the same thing writ large on a people?

That the Holocaust can deliver spiritual and psychological damage to everyone it touches, is evidenced not only by its constant corrosive presence in the Jewish mind, but that many apparent anti-Semitic attacks on Jews have been exposed as hoax attacks by the alleged victims on themselves, driven to madness and strangely compelled to act out this false persecution, presumably to accrue sympathy and legitimise their self-sense of victimhood. Indeed, many Jewish scholars have discussed this need to have an ethnic enemy in terms of a psychological survival strategy to promote group cohesion; and have noted its negative impact on host societies. This toxicity best suggests maintaining a distance from this topic, instead of embracing it; and especially so for children, whether boy or girl, free or slave, Jew and Gentile alike.

The focus on the Holocaust damages Jewish children too, in the same manner as Gentiles; with the additional psychic burden of encouraging them to consider themselves as 4th and 5th generation survivors and reparations seekers. The victimhood chain continues *ad infinitum;*

Unfortunately, the Holocaust is the centrepiece of modern Jewish identity. However, against an ever circling background of Nazi and Hitler claims too often attendant on all public discourse, and the relentless presence of this topic on TV and movies, it risks becoming a major definitional component of our Gentile worldview too. A further consequence of this development is that we increasingly view the last century, and by osmosis much of our own history, through the eyes of another people; moreover, a people who directly express a disappointment with our ethical standards and clearly do not love us. This is especially compromising as the Second World War is our national epic through which we view ourselves positively. That this view now needs nuance may be true, but this must come from within our own ethnic world. The danger to us of allowing others to redefine crucial features of our history in an essentially hostile way is obvious – this is a Judaizing mind melt we could well do without!

If they notice you have an in-group preference they call you White supremacist.

If you notice they have an in-group preference they call you anti-Semitic.

And thusly does the Holocaust tie in with victimhood culture; itself part of this new worldwide moral community that is hostile to us, and increasingly so.

It is not hard to see that school charity initiatives, multiculturalism celebrated, victim centred justice, sexualisation promoted and various tolerances praised, have the same outcome in the mind of the target audience. It denies the child its age of innocence with heaped up woes, calls to action, moral lessons, no cultural pride, only confusion and shame as their lot. And the solution is always the same; circling a bottomless money pit, we see more sanctimony from idiot hypocrites, more government programmes, more public funding, more curricular add-ons, sanction for apostates and the law brought down on the unfavoured.

The Holocaust shows for both victim and victimiser one eternal truth about society – power springs from identity.

In all this the Holocaust plays a crucial role as the keystone of the project, bridging the gap between our little Scottish world to the new global future presumptuously named for Tolerance and Justice. Indeed, the entire social and political order of the contemporary West has evolved to accommodate this supreme king of facts. The alleged virtues of racial diversity and multiculturalism have been erected on the moral foundations of 'the Holocaust.' White nations cannot recognise, far less protect, their own ethnic interests because 'never again.' And for the same 'never again' reason Western nations have an apparent moral obligation to accept unlimited non-White immigration even if it results in their displacement.

By holding together, as it does, in one literally and legally undeniable event, all the in-vogue ideas of racism and intolerance that allegedly plague the Gentile West, the Holocaust is the necessary precursor to enabling the societal stress and cultural lawfare that inevitably follow. Once more the political world hustles from its proper domain to that of our children's well-being.

It is our contention that in primary school our ethical consideration of ourselves as a people should be substantially folkish in the sense of promoting cheerful and self-confident feelings, and that the Jewish moral world brought in through the Holocaust brings the opposite of this – shame, guilt and sadness. As this work notes, our children of whatever background are in no need of additional reminders of misery and injustice.

In the end this curriculum topic is not about foreswearing judgement against others, but ensuring it falls on the proper victim: Us. In this respect, it may be said of a people that if they cannot alter their fate, they can pass it to someone else to suffer. *Thanks, but no thanks!*

With revisionism forever banned, this history is dead. However, the guilt lives forever, as do the reparations – and the ambitions. This is the textbook definition of a racket.

We wish all our readers a happy Rosh Hashanah, Yom Kippur, Passover and Purim!

6
Multiculturism

Mirror, mirror, on the wall,
who's the fairest of them all?

Diversity Is Our Strength,
But Who Is This *Our*?

This chapter is predicated on the observation that there is scarcely an aspect of Western society that has not been subverted to deliberately harm the people who built it, namely, White people; us.

This subversive intent includes the entire political system from local to international, the law in all its manifestations, the entertainment industry, advertising, journalism, mainstream media and – central to our concern – education and academia. And that behind this juggernaut, as the animating power, is a racism industry which finds expression in the multicultural project promoted in our schools. This, like its various comrades-in-arms, the feminist, gender, charity and social justice organisations, all stoke the identity politics furnace with their subliminal message of White guilt and identity confusion. And all this ironically justified by appeals to Western ethical concepts of justice and equality, operating as deniable cover for the true intention, which is not difficult to find as activist professors and media personalities can openly Tweet or blog their future multicultural vision regarding Western nations. Here, in this vision, native Whites are rightly replaced by deserving others; this is apparently necessary for economic reasons, desirable for cultural enhancement and a proper rebuke to our ingrained racism and colonial past. The White nuclear family, it is argued, is the principal force supporting White supremacy and therefore must be 'replaced' for multicultural progress to occur. Sometimes the language used is explicitly genocidal.

In our study we are focusing on the primary school, and schools in general where our argument applies to them – which is often. We appreciate that schools, in common with all our other institutions, did not create the multicultural situation they now find themselves in, and it could be argued that they are just trying to cope as best they can with a complex and confusing situation. This is a fair point, which was mainly true two generations ago at the start of the planned and forced multicultural agenda, but has become less true as time has passed. For in that time our schools have transitioned from multicultural compliance through complicity to stormtroopers of the agenda. They have been encouraged and obliged to do so, of course, and so there is something of the Stockholm Syndrome about this situation; however, we must take them as we find them, and, without question, our schools are full-blown multicultural propaganda factories – and unapologetically so. They have transitioned from recipients of the instructions to the instructors themselves, and are thus now the problem. Now that the infection has taken over the body; our question is, can the body be saved or must it be put out of its misery?

Multiculturalism is a career killing topic and the most anodyne observation, even when coupled with on-board credentials (e.g., garish coloured hair, the accompanying attributes can be easily imagined) brings no protection from hovering swarm of Twitter frauenpolizei. And, as is apparent to anyone who has attempted to engage in a debate on this topic, no amount of caveats and contexts can supply an intellectual forum in which sceptics and advocates can continue the debate, so that even the tiniest consensus is impossible. This is an arena only for furious denouncements. For this reason there is practically no public reference to the current and future implications of multiculturalism within schools. And by this same logic, there is no point in the author even bothering, as a potential defence, to make reasonable, positive and even admiring remarks about other races and cultures, as these will still be utilised as reputation and job killers.[1]

We have then a topic of supreme importance to our children, but our choice as concerned adults in wishing to engage is cheer or be destroyed. This situation is a future tragedy in the making, as dissent driven underground eventually comes back angry from its lair.

We're all one big family in our school
and equally proud of all the cultures we contain.

So they say on the school website. But they would say so, wouldn't they? But why claim 'equally proud'; methinks this unnecessary qualification inadvertently reveals evidence of doubt, even, dare you think it, of its opposite? Considering these statements forensically reveals an insecurity about their acceptance; one can only claim 'equally' if there is, in fact, a ranking; and if there is a ranking, what is its true scale? The false optimism, and frankly sometimes desperate need for approval, found in school multicultural statements indicates too strong a need to persuade, which is always a cover for an untruth. When things are self-evidently true, one doesn't need to keep repeating them. This constant banging of the multicultural drum (or tom tom!) shows the establishment fear of people reaching the 'wrong' conclusion in balancing cost against benefits. It's as if:

The true measure of a school's legitimacy
is its diversity record.

Drilling into the 'pride' implications, our emotionally grounded and meme savvy ethnic-others reach the bedrock of White gesture politics – that the 'pride' is a suppliant gesture of White guilt, tacked onto a weak-willed need to placate. And, as usual with political celebrations, the deeper psychology reveals its opposite – the racism they deny. And the roar of lies is deafening for those with ears to hear. This more accurate reading will be carried forward and transmitted to their children, whose based ethnic self-interest outsmarts their White peers by an order of magnitude.

There are those who claim that to discuss costs and benefits attributable to ethnic-others is to mark them for special attention, and is thus inherently racist. For, regardless of origin, once domiciled here they have the same entitlements as everyone else, and therefore no further need to justify themselves.[2]

That they constantly need to do so, however, is a recognition of the mainly silent resistance to multiculturalism among us ethnic natives and an attempt to balance the clear, and probably never-ending, costs of accommodation.[3] These points bring out the contradictions inherent in multiculturalism; one cannot say that the ethnic-others bring a universal advantage, but they also need privileged access to resources and other special concessions. For this privileged access, in conferring an advantage on some, is a net disadvantage to everyone else. So then, it becomes clear; everyone else is *us*, and the *our* in 'Multiculturalism is our strength', is actually *them*. Considered clearly, this endlessly repeated mantra is a lie.

Access to White people is not a human right.

To get around the turmoil that would be attendant on claims of parasitism and privilege, advanced and denied respectively, but once spoken loud never to be retracted, our educational system becomes wise like the three monkeys that neither hear, see and, especially, say anything. Bottling things up like this, of course, only works for a while.

In any case, most advocates for a multicultural school world argue it as a net benefit to all, and the arguments in this chapter are contingent on this claim. That some individuals may benefit in some way from multicultural presence is not at issue, for this must be true. However, our concern is with the impact on the whole school community, with particular consideration to the native White stock. That's me and mine.

Our Scope

It is my intention to discuss the practical impact of multiculturalism on primary schools, and not discuss the origin and nature of our obligations as hosts, nor critique the wider phenomenon in society. However, this impact is hardly a stand-alone topic, for schools are not just the chosen playground for multicultural political ambitions, but a future demographic window into how such ambitions will play out in society a generation from now. We can expect, then, that the feedback loops between school and the wider culture will muddy my intended focus, but better reflect the true nature of this transformation.[4] Basically, then, as far as this topic is concerned, you may run and hide, but the political and ethical issues will hunt you down.

Mwaa, wwaa…aahhh. Arghhh!

Chewbacca

('I love going to Drumchapel Primary School. Its multicultural vibrancy feels just like the Mos Eisley Cantina.' Translated from Wookiee-Glaswegian by Chewie's classroom PSA)

The practical outcomes claimed for multiculturalism in primary schools are the same as for wider society, with only a few alterations for scale and institutional peculiarities; and, of course, minus the alleged economic necessity of importing others.[5] Schools supposedly enjoy the obvious benefits of direct exposure to other cultures and languages, dietary variety and the sunny dispositions and life-affirming presence of disparate ethnic-others, approvingly referred to as vibrancy.

In this view, native stock children are especial beneficiaries; their experience of school typically being described as enriched. We note that this phrase is seldom used ironically! Irony is also absent when it is noted that the multicultural school prepares the White pupil for the global future. Such a future presumably including, although seldom mentioned, the coming demographic adjustments to, eventually, minority status. (Check Sweden for how quickly this can occur.) This reality obliges the admittance of some funding reallocation difficulties due to 'disparate learning outcomes' (as remedial and language needs are addressed) and occasional unfortunate issues[6] attendant upon the levelling process between 'different culturally conditioned ways of behaving', although the latter are often attributed to the intolerance or ignorance of the native stock children, their parents and culture. But certainly never to different psychological profiles with respect to the causal issues, which may include propensity to aggression, deceit, querulousness, focus, conscientiousness, or self-aggrandisement – even if such a thing was clearly evident. Any evidence of this would be buried, or would be yet again ascribed to systemic racism. I know that you know this!

We are to believe that nothing is worse than racism, nothing – except anti-Semitism.

The view we are countering, then, sees ethnic-others as if they are White people with darker skin, who have essentially the same societal values relating to trust, orderliness, morality, gratitude, religiosity, intellectual appetency, ambition, etc., as ourselves. So ingrained are our variants of these values in our collective consciousness that we seldom consider them as unique, nor imagine that others could, equally unthinkingly, see things differently. Instead, believing, in our conceit, that our sharing of the same basic human values is a sufficient basis for proceeding successfully with the multicultural project; imagining our psychological and cultural differences, not as fundamental aspects of separate historical and racial evolution that cannot be simply accommodated to new settings, but as the little things that enhance this new wonderful multicultural future world. The incidents in Rotherham *et al.*, however, have demonstrated that many of our Western concepts, even of the most basic character, such as the value of human life, can have zero value to others; not just as individuals, but as a community. Just as we lack the ability to consider ourselves as a people and a unique race, so too it appears to be difficult for the White mind to grasp the sometimes visceral mental world of the tribal mind. Their default characteristics are not ours, and the differences are not simple things to see, define and accept, far less celebrate. Imagine how the multicultural debate in schools would develop should this, arguably more worldly view, become accepted as the default assumption among native Whites about the replacement population living amongst then?

We, that being us and not them, are expected to accept *a priori* that the previously above claimed benefits are essentially true and substantially real; that they are, in other words, actual benefits. And that their acceptance as such has been established beyond doubt and so further consideration on this topic can proceed with the so-called benefits as an established foundation. However, it would be incorrect to accept them without evidence, for these foundational multicultural propositions can easily be examined. Let us do so. Firstly, who says they are benefits and specifically how so?

The reader here knows that, even at this starting point, already the frauenpolizei are reaching for their holstered smart phones; light thickens and the R word makes wing to the blackening ether.[7]

The Benefits of Multicultural Schools

This Happy Breed

So, what exactly is the benefit of exposure to other cultures and languages in a school setting? Specifically what? Here at the start of our investigation we find that the argument advanced commits the logical fallacy of assuming what it is required to prove; and replies with a tautology, the multicultural mix is just better because… it just is! If evidence was demanded, the claim would just be reiterated in slightly different form. And seemingly made truer by being seen on large school posters and waved on parades by screeching fem-puppets. As if the large letters used actually do make the eponymous *us* stronger, just by being bigger!

Certainly, there is interest, and often a certain joy, just in seeing how differently constituted others live their lives. But, depending as it is on novelty, the compare and contrast is usually short lived. So racially or historically bound are our habits of thought and action, that even well-admired alternatives fronted by outgroup others seldom make the leap to full acceptance. Generally, after a while, one tires of outgroup others and come to resent the necessary adjustments one has to make to their foreign habits and languages,[8] hence the reason it is so good to be back home after a foreign sojourn. This same implicit feeling travels both ways, of course, and builds tension into the system from the start.

There is often some aspect of other cultures that one admires; however, in the school context these aspects, by logic, should be limited to school specific attributes, for example, a supportive family structure, 'respect for learning' or good manners. Such claims, being entirely subjective, are seldom strongly founded, and run the risk of being considered patronising. However, even if certain attributes were widely accepted as true, one would still be left with the problem of describing specifically how the school system as a whole is benefitted.

In consideration of these arguments we need not limit such claimed benefits to direct academic evidence, such as raising maths attainment, etc; for, as we have argued in this work for secondary and tertiary effects to be considered, so here too such multicultural benefits could be downstream effects of particular cultural differences or behavioural attributes. Freely thinking of possible effects, these could be providing useful or unusual insights, work and behaviour templates, or unique parental contributions. This should be the point in the debate at which powerful evidence would kill the multicultural gainsayers, but instead of the strong hand played, we have the weak hand bluffed. Multicultural advocates are not able to provide any concrete evidence because there is none. Ethnic others generally coming as supplicants from cultures whose school traditions and study habits offer no improvements to our own, or are otherwise not transferable (e.g., certain ethnic groups are academically very driven and results oriented, but this is a study template unacceptable to European notions of family balance and child welfare).

We must note that others come here and place their children within our school system because of a benefit to them and theirs; bringing improvements to our system, or to us personally, is not remotely a concern, and we really should not be surprised if no net benefit accrues to us. This argument would, of course, be different if the children of a peer or superior competitor culture would arrive in flooding numbers from, say, Japan, or an extra-terrestrial location; with such pupils bringing exemplary classroom habits of self-discipline, or specialist knowledge of interstellar propulsion systems.

In fairness to such others, they themselves seldom make such claims of bringing benefits,[9] this service being provided by multicultural activists, globalist-inspired organisations and co-opted school teachers. All usually White, at least on the outside.

Wonderful Others from Sunnier Climes

We have been encouraged to believe that the mere presence of ethnic-others brings benefits via their innate wonderfulness. This quality is never made explicit, nevertheless, our news, advertising and political commentators drum out this message by suggestion and inference; and TV shows and movies favourably depict for us our multicultural future.[10] Our children see and hear this every day and are supposed to assume, if White, that they are lucky to have such wonderful others among us. And that questioning such is a taboo, indeed, it is evil to even think of such a question. In real life, however, it is we ethnic natives that are the desired presence. And we only ever needed ourselves to make our future work; this fact partly explains the relentless nature of this sunshine message as a necessary pre-emptive counter to the eventual development of a more nuanced, if not hostile, view of multiculturalism. The ethnic bonus of multiculturalism in our schools is, then, actually provided by we Whites and not for us by ethnic-others, who (honestly) bring basically nothing outside of the range that we already had. This is not a criticism, but observed reality. Coming here to live amongst the tolerant and kindly us, and access freely our education system for their children, should be like a dream come true. One could fairly assume that such beneficiaries of our largesse (and our ancestors' patrimony) would result in them counting their blessings every day and not their grievances. Instead, some have come to consider their presence here (and not without some justification given the action of Western governments and NATO) as a revenge mission.

Fairly considered as individuals, our new citizens occupy the same range of school-significant attributes as White Euro children; these being related to agreeableness, educability, focus, honesty, aggressiveness, self-control, sociability, happiness and respectfulness. Considered collectively, however, the picture changes to something less certain, and especially so if one factors in intelligence; although it is not permitted to mention, far less consider, this queenly attribute and so I won't.[11]

We adults know that the British multicultural world we see presented in the various media we consume does not reflect social reality. It is likewise in schools; the ethnic others are just children, and bring nothing special by virtue of their otherness. And it does the multicultural cause no favour to encourage the belief that there is some magic in their presence, as if happy Munchkins or darker coloured Smurfs. For this picaninny-level fiction, on meeting reality is seen for what it is – propaganda. And once propaganda is outed, cynicism and resentment follow. However, such is the coercive power of multiculturalist shibboleths, one must behave as if this magic other is true. This is part of the mental gymnastics occasioned by living with the inherent contradictions of the multicultural world.

Here we are not arguing for the opposite; claiming that ethnic-others, by virtue of their culture, necessarily bring hostile dispositions and a class-disrupting presence, although they of course may as individuals.[12] It may be conceded, however, that a surly and combative attitude could likely be a future outcome in school, this filtering down from developments in wider society; such as, continuing forced association, empowerment legislation and pushback against the same, and the presence of endless racism claims whipped up by journalist hate-mongers. Thus illustrating the Iron Law of Unintended Consequences – that is, if they were unintended!

The Celebrations

The presence of many other spoken languages in school is claimed as a benefit. It is certainly the subject of much celebration if not outright boasting, pride being evoked,[13] as if this number somehow reflects favourably on schools, although they are merely the passive recipients of such speakers. However, examined for specifics, we find no advantage to schools, unless seeing hello written in scores of languages posted on 'Our Values' wall is the advantage!

Global World Sceptic: *How is speaking thirty-five different languages in your school a good thing to be celebrated?*

Global World Head Teacher Advocate: *Well, because,... emmm. You're just a Nazi. No free speech to Nazis!*

Admittedly, there is a usefulness in one's own life of being able to speak other languages, however, I believe that this has been conflated with a benefit to the whole institution. Sometimes a claim is made of an institutional gain, as a kind of intellectual boost, by means of cross-cultural references, analogous thinking enhanced or witty forms of expression, but this is realistically the preserve of adult multilingual intellectuals or TV characters, and is thus virtually never heard in school, except perhaps as an occasional comment by a highly intelligent child or by accidental happenstance.

The other languages are, then, only spoken among their native speakers to their sometimes-intentional self-exclusion, and are not otherwise taught or of wider relevance to the curriculum. They thus represent no advantage to the school as an institution, or to ethnic Scottish or British children, or other monoglot English speakers.

The celebration is, in fact, an instruction to celebrate.

Conversely, one could argue that no significant disadvantage accrues to the children of a class if some classmate, whether by choice or necessity, speaks a separate language in that class. This is basically true, up to the point where the situation compromises progress in lessons. However, even before this situation is obvious, a subtle degradation of lesson quality can still occur, as we shall subsequently see. For even those ethnic-other children whose English is seemingly fluent, typically prove on closer familiarity to be less so. In any case, the presence of such children still does not represent an advantage to ethnic native English-speaking classmates, or to the school in general.

The Tower of Babel Revisited

Most of the direct disadvantages arise from the need to devote resources to correct the English language deficit suffered by other first language speakers, and the attendant impact of this on lessons and general topic progress; in some classes this can be very significant and those other native English-speaking pupils who suffer from this situation have to do so in silence – as do their parents, excepting the occasional remarks at parent's night which are best discretely forgotten. Even wonderfully bilingual children, whose English is at otherwise native level, still suffer in certain deficiencies in the appreciation of Scotch saws, figures of speech, humorous intent, peculiar analogies and similar culturally specific features; this situation contains the possibility of a limiting effect on the teacher's ability to naturally approach a topic and would, of course, increase as the number of such children increases.

As the number of children requiring remedial language services increases, as the demographic trends show, so will the quality of such services further decrease, which will in turn further stress the system elsewhere, while driving up ancillary costs. This will create lower levels of actual attainment, lead to more claims and counter-claims of teacher incompetence, systemic racism and political betrayal which will obviously be stoked by those interested to do so – these being the same who brought about this situation. This will lead, as it always has, to manipulation of outcomes to mimic promised improvements, or to highlight supposed prejudice with a view to levering an advantage. Thus we see that multicultural grievances will add to an already well-established, anti-meritocratic trend contained within the drive for equal outcomes; here the bright and diligent must keep pace with the obtuse and undisciplined.

Calls for increased ethnic inclusion into the teaching profession to address the 'betrayal' of ethnic children, freshen up a 'stale' (i.e., White) profession and increase societal fairness, etc., etc., will result in further lowering of standards to ensure that such inclusion targets are met, this resulting in an obvious further impact on actual standards and more claims of institutional racism. As well as certain added social, legal and employment complexities as a result of an influx such teachers into the school labour force – this is the whirlpool's spin prior to the flush.

The impact on spoken and written Standard English, and the teaching of national culture, cannot avoid being altered for the worst by this process. Not least by the calls for 'inclusive' (which actually means exclusive) literature, further driving a wedge between our English language past, present and future. Already, there are claims that Standard English is racist, in that it promotes so-called White standards which 'deny the language experience of people of colour', etc. Naturally, then, this argument continues, in the interests of equity, English grammar and spelling should be replaced by something less rigorous and more in keeping with the manner of the unlearned and ignoramuses who advocate for this. The inner desolation we experience at the thought of the loss of our glorious language would be matched, not only by the joy amongst multicultural advocates of such a loss, but ironically by the inability to express it anyway. What we have, then, is in actuality a call for Newspeak; the natural language of the weaponised rabble.

Further On Up the Road

Meanwhile, as these first-order effects work their way through the system, the second order effects wait ahead for their welcome. This will come when speakers of other languages reach a certain percentage of the school community and, of course, the future wider community. The languages celebrated under multiculturalism are thusly validated, and validation demands its price as a right. That right ratchets up the recognition with its incorporation into school policy and funding for alternative language lessons and literature, perhaps even further and separate demands, for example, remedial lessons in the home language,[14] with claims and lawsuits following on the back of the inevitable disappointment with this process. One can hardly say to a separate home language speaker that their home language is worthy of celebration and pride without there being consequences in how that speaker comes to consider their own language and its cultural position within the host language culture – and particularly so when such speakers reach a critical mass. Pride demands its rights and, as these will now exist in opposition to the host language (i.e., Standard English and Scotch), the stage is set for confrontation over space and resources. The host culture inevitably seeing, to their great chagrin, system gaming and successful racial lawfare waged against what they regard as their patrimony. In contrast, the ethnic-others, powered and justified by earlier celebration and pride, logically seeing their own claims as equally valid; for this will be their country too. This is a part of the culture war that will be waged across many domains, for expression of culture readily translates to expression of grievances. Demographics then come into play; school communities split (but secretly, at least at first, due to fear of doxing and racial legislation), management appointments become exclusively political and everyone loses in this fight, but especially the children by becoming proxies for the wider struggle. It is at this point that one finally discovers that social trust and community capital were all along features of homogenous societies.

Another future consequence of second-language pride is the creation of separate language communities within schools. This has not happened in Scotland, but with the coming demographic changes it is reasonable to expect it; indeed, it has already occurred elsewhere.[15] This development would further reinforce group and ethnic preferences on all sides, and allow among other language speakers for a separate and secret communication channel which would come to be used, not just for reinforcing identity and intentional self-exclusion from the host culture, but contains the potential for encouraging disrespectful remarks to teachers and other pupils. This I have witnessed.

The end of this is that school language culture must change, and, consequently, the literature used for the enculturalisation of children. Scotland then becomes a different Scotland, to the pride and celebration (presumably, at least of their victory) of the globalist Sanhedrin and their droids. Perhaps, as an exercise in dystopian whimsy, we may imagine that in some not-so-distant futurescape, English itself will become even more hybridised, like the Cityspeak spoken in the futuristic movie *Bladerunner*. Although in our case, a heady, swear-loving mix of Glaswegian Urdu, Polski-español and chip shop Pidgin. Hopefully, this development would make tweeting more inclusive.[16]

The Restaurant Theory

That dull, grey Britain had its cuisine transformed by multiculturalism seems basically true, although the exclusive goodness of this development and whether it would have happened anyway is another question. With respect to schools catering to multicultural palates or surrendering to demands, as the case may be, the first order effects of such exotic variety could be weakly argued as being a good thing for gastronomic reasons, and as a demonstration of good manners by providing dishes that satisfy the fussy tastes of our former guests and now future co-citizens. And perhaps too, on a practical level, more a case of avoiding complaints, lawsuits, the R word and, thusly, the primary school equivalent of a jailhouse dining hall riot.[17]

This claim is only weakly argued for, because of my familiarity with the various exotically inspired selections served, which it would be fair to say do not do the original homeland cuisine much justice. Although this remark is not intended to be especially disparaging – a little would be sufficient for my purpose – as it is in the nature of such school dishes to be budget oriented and the nature of children to choose childishly if given the choice, so pasta and pizza, but no vindaloo or boiled monkey.

The effects further down the lunch line are of two sorts:

The one attendant on the high carbohydrate (rice and pasta) content of such dishes, and their long range metabolic consequences of obesity and diabetes – as can readily be seen by the flabby and disproportioned shapes of those who prioritise such fare. By providing such fodder schools further normalise this ruinous diet, and then further endorse it by curriculum activities focused on this and other nutritional canards. Admittedly, schools are merely following the erroneous, Big Food inspired, public policy in this.

The second effect is the establishment of a principle, reasonable on the face of it, that it is correct to offer variety and make dietary concessions to others' tastes or religious requirements. Once built into the system, as it is, the eventual consequences are more of the same with its corollary of extra cost, lower quality and complaint weaponised by multicultural considerations. If you do X for her, then why not Y for me? This principle will naturally extend to other areas of school life. Variety concessions and complaints feed off each other, metastasising throughout the institution until it is lost to chaos. The counter-argument that this claim is overstated may be mostly true at the moment, but abstract principles have real-life consequences. If halal and vegetarian, why not kosher, vegan and fruitarian? Why not a separate dining area for a protected group? Garlic eaters table, personal cutlery, chopsticks on demand? Why not anything? The end point of this argument is that, once empowered, kindly concessions gets met with insistent demands. And all the problems of too many concessions to choice, mated to customer empowerment, lead to a situation of constant dissatisfaction. Bureaucratic inertia, political interference and funding limitations will ensure that the lunch and snack aspect of public education will forever disappoint, with the final result being that the potential for exotic revival of British school fare will come down to more carbohydrate – the exact opposite of what our children should be eating. The quality of the food, though, will be the least of the issues, as this situation eventually realises its potential as a sideshow campaign in the school's culture and race war.

Considered as a menu, the multicultural food benefit to school is a non-starter.

Second-order Effects: Thoughtcrime

Many of the second order effects are to do with social and psychological consequences of the policing, and self-policing, of speech and thought. And the further transmission of such codes, mostly tacitly, but sometimes directly in specific lessons concerned with school multicultural and so-called anti-racist initiatives. Ethnic-others read the over-compensation of White society at large as a confirmation of racism, not its denial. Here, we are reminded of

Hamlet's mother, Queen Gertrude, who famously noted that one can protest too much, methinks.

And while it is a good thing to be sensitive to the dignity and feelings of others, one can easily go too far with this intention if one becomes too deferential and goes beyond what would be a normal level of reciprocation obliged from the other. Then, instead of good-will, one generates resentment. And, also runs the danger of inadvertently signalling weakness to a hidden predator, indeed one can even stimulate such behaviour; for weakness and supplication invite predation.

So, on the one side, the promotion of multiculturalism in our schools as an exclusively good thing runs up against an observable reality that this is not always the case. However, in the current climate even such a thought becomes a crime, hence the earlier reference to thoughtcrime from Orwell's *1984*. The sanctions attendant upon the thoughtcrime being expressed, or even implied, result in it being supressed, mainly by self-policing. This, in turn, generates a resentment that feeds what it was supposed to prevent. This burden applies exclusively to Whites. Other ethnicities, activists and race-hustlers can publicly express disparaging, even genocidal, remarks directed at the White population and escape consequence. There is no downside to publicly hating White people; indeed, by being openly anti-White the most mediocre of journalists can readily find top dollar employment and be feted on the BBC. Children are well aware of this situation by upper primary and get their daily school fix of proper racial protocol via BBC Newround. One could argue that younger children are shielded from such concerns by their lack of understanding and that this claim therefore exaggerates the danger. However, I would contend that this is to confuse their immaturity with insensitivity. For the actual situation with infants is the reverse, in that they soak up (as Mother Nature intended) the multicultural atmosphere which is awash with concerns and racial tropes. They don't need to literally understand to get the message, they intuit it. Indeed, this is how infants learn about their culture and its forbidden zones.

The children on the other side of the multicultural divide, are exposed to the constant drumbeat that they and their ethnic interests are needful of protection from institutionally entrenched, bigoted nativist Whites. What psychic hinterland must those children inhabit and what thoughtcrimes pass through their minds? Of course, this understanding more describes their near future, for while at primary school they are still processing all this information, as yet unaware that their sense of themselves is gradually being weaponised against the host society. The worm is planted, and this cannot make for an open and happy environment.

Children cannot be expected to understand all this as a concept, but they don't need to. They understand what's going on and, with their enhanced emotional sensibility as nature's compensation for their intellectual deficit, they pick up on the codes and act them out. Every day our schools provide templates, reinforced by MSM news, of how this situation plays out and the role one is obliged to adopt. Those children who grasp this early – being a bully while playing the victim, reflexively accusing classmates of racism and even (author witnessed) White supremacy – act as exemplars of how the game is to be played to their ethnic peers. Well taught at seven!

Were We Really So Bigoted?

The apparent replacement of good manners by codes and policies was not a natural or necessary evolution, either in schools or in the wider society, but a deliberate attempt to weaponise social relations. By this we mean that the potential for official complaint, even for minor or unintended infringements, now resides with the super-sensitive, as well as malcontents, offence-seekers, race warriors, idiots, harassers and nuisance legal claimants. This problem was nowhere near the size it was claimed to be by the justice activists, who exaggerated,[18] and even manufactured, spurious examples to be placed in the mainstream media, or as portrayed in countless TV shows and movies featuring cardboard cut-out White racists; all in order to achieve the legislation they desired.[19] Hate speech laws, for example can easily be seen as both a tool (in this case, a hammer) of the 'racial grievance' and 'social justice' industries and a legal scam targeting Whites; and who cannot have failed to notice the ethnicity of the lawyers running this scam. Noticing this, we see further that diversity is a mask for racial identity politics, and that multiculturalist activism is the leading edge of a larger ideological campaign to shape attitudes on a wide range of societal issues, but especially those connected to the White family.

The use of such laws creates the very febrile atmosphere that they claim to be resisting. Everything that happens in this arena provides the legitimisation for more of the same and a template for future grievances. Indeed, the scope for such is everywhere and everything. It is not difficult to find claims that the entirety of life in the West is racist, along with philosophy, religion, democracy, logic, science, art, music, history and so on. Even rational discourse has been identified as an expression of White oppression; admittedly such claims are gratuitously inflammatory, as well as insane, but nevertheless those making them are readily given a platform (typically in MSM or academia) to do so. And today's insanity is tomorrow's orthodoxy! Quietly, conscious of needing deniability, topics that connect with European excellence (e.g., historical architecture, scientific achievement, great artists and thinkers, etc.) are avoided, sometimes even unconsciously for fear of seeming chauvinist, or of mocking others by comparison with their clearly inferior cultural equivalent.

This, then, is the multicultural school background within which our children will grow, and evolve an understanding of themselves as either victim or oppressor, guilty or innocent. Thusly are they welcomed into the world of 'collective guilt' and 'universal grievance', both simultaneously running through every classroom and every child. Certain groups are experts at dishing out this mindfuck and we Whites are unfortunate in being the unwitting pupils of the best hating, and self-hating, group in the history of the world.

This is the implicit message to our children; guilt and righteous anger respectively. If you are White you represent a culture that historically and currently practices a heinous racism that never seems to lessen. And if you are other-raced, you are the recipient of this apparently motiveless injustice that can easily be found embedded within any and every situation, even (especially?) innocent remarks. This same situation would allow, should you wish to avail yourself of it, to shift the blame for any sort of failure or disappointment to the racism of the host society; or even better, one can boost the complaint by means of intersectionality – the power obtained by synergistically combining fashionable complaints (fat shaming, queer-negative language, sexism, anti-Islam, etc.) into a single package. Indeed, in this view, one's entire history can be regarded as one of oppression by the very country and race you now live among. The apparent truth of this excess of White hate demonstrated by the ever-increasing legislation, school policy and classroom programmes designed to thwart it. Like a darker angelic presence, Righteous Revenge hangs over the classroom, ready to smite alike the seven-year-old White girl and 58-year-old head teacher should they speak heresy towards this latter day religion. Or even think (too loudly?) why so many people want to come here to be victims of White supremacy and systemic racism. This trend ends in the creation of a Race Offenders Registry. Or, more rather, its new retributive stage begins here in denial to apostates of public services, banking and employment. Already such action is spoken of as a condign punishment for racists, and the MSM and political activists are prepping the public mind for acceptance of such.

With its implied guilt hovering over too many ordinary everyday social interactions, and empowered malcontents with mobile phones always ready, our children then will grow up policing themselves or face being policed by the police. No one likes being told what to think, or of living in a world where they are constrained and endangered by policies and laws that were apparently designed to stop them doing what they had no intention of doing anyway. And so, for protection against false claims, no doubt a technological solution will be offered (or more properly, proffered!) and then accepted; for there is never any lack of appetite for increasing the power of surveillance! (This, of course, will not end in the classroom, but the bathroom.) No doubt too, some pupils will be freelancing to social media as circumstances, and the potential for LOLs and lawsuits, dictate.

This generates resentment which festers in the individual and corrodes social relations, leading people away from embracing the wider community and back to the only true safe space of family and tribe. And in the perverse hinterland of the human mind, what is denied becomes compelling. A heightened racial awareness is driven to the front of the mind, evidence of racism is found everywhere, and spinning off from this, challenge and confrontation arises. But, with the policies and laws, and with racial aggravationists in place, this cannot end where it started; perhaps simply and with apologies all round. But instead, dipped from the public purse, incomes for lawyers and ultimately costed to our well-being. And with each case concluded, the legal and policy aspects of multiculturalism are ratcheted forward.

And so, of necessity, even of safety, in the increasingly coercive multicultural regime foisted on us, where everything segues to race, Whites, at last, are forced to consider themselves, and their interests, racially – and may well become, and unapologetically so, the actual racists they were originally so egregiously labelled.

Every Remark Carries Potential for a Racial Interpretation.

The school becomes a place of paradoxes; different ethnicities getting on well as they usually do at first, and then increasingly discovering, as they are increasingly reminded of race, preferences which run the risk of not being interpreted neutrally: resources claimed or gamed, funding diverted according to political agenda and legal risk, celebrations compromised to ensure 'proper' balance, false reporting required and thus integrity compromised by thusly compromised staff, which further chases out men.[20] When even sandwiches and 300 year old paintings can be claimed as objects of race hate, there is no limit to the politicisation of previously neutral topics as race sensitivity inevitably becomes a part of every lesson. Teachers themselves run the risk of every remark carrying the potential of a racial interpretation adding further stress. Even holiday treats run this risk.[21]

Chocolate buttons: *That's rayciss!*

White chocolate buttons: *That's White supremacist!*

No chocolate buttons: *Reparations required!*

This, in turn, leads to calls for funding for more 'specialists' and courses to correct the claimed institutional racism, which claim is tacitly justified by the presence of the courses and specialist in the first place! This funding falsely diverted is lost to the common good forever, but forever contributes to the issue it is supposed to correct. It must also be noted, as we have done before in this work, that too often such experts are of HR pedigree and so are only experts in their own useless world; indeed, even worse, they are often the badly motivated, self-hater wymmen one would expect to gravitate to such projects. It is a disgrace that, by virtue of the courses they are employed to run, the authority of a pedagogue is conferred upon them – for never was it less deserved. The financial and time-wasted costs of such meaninglessness qualifications are, however, the least cost to us, for this credentialism damages the entire credibility of the academic system and that of those teachers who are obliged to be so certificated. This situation is the cash hustle part of the multicultural-academic complex and is simply a vast fraud.[22] However, let us be clear, this money was not wasted. It was stolen!

The money spent on anti-racism workshops was not wasted. It was stolen!

The ideological dominance of multiculturalism brings a whole set of managerial and legal problems that extend out from and back into the school; the speech codes, dress codes, hate speech laws, religious requirements, anti-harassment and anti-discrimination regulations and forced association have led to the rise of dogmatic managerial systems in which integrity has no place. A teacher will be sacrificed on the altar of multiculturalism should any grievance arise involving an ethnic-other family. Thus this situation makes cowards of us and accelerates us further into such systemic cowardice by promoting to management the same cowards, specifically because they are cowards and can be reliably trusted to redirect any blame back down the chain to the teachers.

More laws, less trust; less trust, less social credit; less social credit, more tribal thinking. And then the big questions that should have been asked at the beginning of this multicultural process arrive, but this time not as abstract issues, but concrete ones directly connected to your child's welfare in their school life and beyond: *What about my kids?*

The answer, as I witnessed a new Swede telling an original ethnic Swede: *If you don't like it here any more* [Sweden], *then go somewhere else.*[23]

Anti-racism:
Scottish Education's Number One Priority

Each year 'Show Racism the Red Card Scotland' holds a competition that sees young people, from Primary 1 to FE, coming up with creative ways to promote messages of anti-racism.

But why? How did this become so important? Did those promoting this not see the implicit dark message, or notice the terrible potential with the transformation of the definitions of racism from what one does, to what one says, to what one thinks, to what one is assumed to think, to presence, to mere existence being a hate crime if you have the wrong opinion. Or colour; and here we arrive at 'Whiteness', the latest Talmudic sophistry which allows the attack on White interests and Whites as people under the justice trope of merely attacking a concept. Primary schools are not *yet* discussing 'Whiteness'[24] as a pathology to be eradicated and then celebrated as a good for humanity. However, this morbid obsession is in the background to all the cultural choices made within school which have gradually undermined White cultural interests. For example, it is now a near-necessity that no Christian religious festival can be mentioned without an obsequious reference to some other religion's apparently equivalent festival (e.g., Hanukkah and Christmas). This is a phenomenon that flows just one way.

What is worrying about this particular aspect of our anti-racism priority is that, under the guise of due consideration to other cultural practices, the gradual erosion of White cultural references tacitly signals their irrelevance. The child not seeing or hearing of such references naturally assumes they do not exist, or are otherwise of no value; and there are, alas, few school-based sources to disabuse them of this notion.

This requirement to promote others as equally valid reduces the preference the native culture is due by right, and thus shows it disrespect. In doing this, the disrespect rebounds back on native Whites who cannot, or at least do not, defend and high honour their own cultural practices and icons. This is another example of the observation that in attempting to respect everything equally regardless of intrinsic merit, or to celebrate everything equally, is to respect and celebrate nothing in particular. This akin to not actually celebrating at all!

In this context to preference one thing is to disfavour something else. To honour a culture more than your own is to dishonour your own. To dishonour your own in front of ethnic-others is to be a traitor. To always be seeking equivalences as appeasement, to always be apologising, to be always finding validity through the well-being of other groups, signals weakness. This cultural relativism further damages our native confidence in our own values, as it bolsters the same effect in the field of ethics and morality; accepting all values as equal in truth and validity makes it impossible to defend your own. One thusly destroys one's own authority and source of power. Only Whites do this. Teaching self-hate is our White intellectual patrimony!

Without a doubt, then, there should indeed be a focus on anti-racism in Scottish primary schools. The reader is by now sure to understand the direction in which this should be encouraged to flow.

**Race is not everything,
but without it everything is nothing.**

The tertiary effects for ethnic Scots (and those sympathetically inclined others) must be eventually devastating, and it is here that we come to the original vision which led us to this situation; be lesser, then be gone! Our high culture, the envy and emulation of the world, is misrepresented as racist, and then additional isms are tagged on as specifically required by the situation. Next, our literature and history are inevitably reduced to accommodate the supposed exclusion of others, and then they are disprized, with the curse on it returned to us in loss of self. This is a process comparable to that which occurred relatively recently in our history with Gaelic culture; a loss which is puzzled over by patriots and lamented by all, and not just those who have the blood: How could we have let this happen, is the refrain repeated in countless books, poems and especially songs; yet, here we go again, and achieved the same way, through the children in school and by replacement; although this time by an order of magnitude faster.

Multicultural memes only exist to destroy the host culture.

Our language and literature are the foundations of our culture and of our proper conceit of ourselves, and too the crucial connection to our past of our ancestors whose sacrifices and talents led to the wealth creation that we surrender today. Honouring your ancestors and their achievements is not only the respectful thing to do, and thus self-respectful, but in maintaining the link from the past one also invests in the future; this is as your ancestors wished. This is why it is a Biblical commandment.

We surrender too much when we surrender any aspect of this patrimony to political correctness, for we have seen that this process started has no limit, each concession involving our cultural achievements, results in further attacks on the rump. This is the logic of a running retreat, eventually one runs out of space and treasure to surrender. Unless one turns to face this foe, the attacks continue for ever and ever until we are no one and nothing – thus Europe dies and does not even know why! And yet while we are encouraged, or even forced, to take away and thus render invisible any positive and beautiful reminders of our past; ethnic-others are encouraged and funded to celebrate theirs. This situation is so crude in its execution that one is apt to consider it as a direct challenge to us.

Celebration of European culture reminds ethnic-others of their alien status, and it is not unreasonable to assume that, having no claim of kinship with European civilisation, they would neutrally regard its continuing immiseration via multicultural pressures. While others – resentful at their suppliant position in our country, constantly aggrieved by racism claims and perhaps mindful, correctly or not, of the destructive role of the West in their former homelands – in the deep working of their collective mind actively welcome this process. Some clearly enjoy the dismantling of cultural sources of White identity and pride, psychologically considering it as a revenge tribute; it is not difficult to find frank statements of such, often by holders of political office and various academics, including those involved in education. Sometimes this deep hate is projected directly to native Whites, claimed as their hate returned, and sometimes it is disguised by the sophistry of 'Whiteness', as already noted. All ethnic-other children are exposed to this febrile atmosphere, and we could expect their default attitude to European glory to range from indifference to antipathy.

White children need to hear about their inherited cultural excellence.

The tragedy for our children is not that the ignorant, self-excluded and jealous should dismiss our greatness, but that many Scottish or British teachers themselves are, by education or inclination, not only unable to champion their own high culture, but can be uninterested in doing so. (J.S Bach ❦126 votes)

This should be a cause for shame and a desire for correction, but is instead considered, if considered at all, as a blow against the patriarchy or the like; alas, the deranged idea that our high culture is a morbid expression of oppressive dead White men is common currency in the femcentric circles that many teachers inhabit. This way of thinking is generally an unthinking one, in that the intelligent women who largely comprise the profession seldom consider the propositions that underlie the globalist worldview, having not been equipped with the rhetorical tools to do so. Their celebration of other cultures, and unwitting denigration of their own, is, then, best understood as a programmed default. And, as we have argued elsewhere in this work in relation to other social justice ambitions, it is not an accident that many teachers think thusly. Indeed, being prepared as 'dumb terminals', as if with processing ability limited to that necessary for receiving and transmitting globalist and diversity instructions, is as central to the success of the multicultural project as is the distractive power of the fetid poptrash online world and the demonic role models they have been exposed to in their rearing.

O Lord, protect our children from the fury
of the multiculturalists!

There is, however, another danger posed by such teachers; many of them dream of being part of a world-transforming enterprise. This, having been inculcated by their own education, is believed to be the highest realisation of female emancipation and self-expression. Indeed, some even claim that the most important and enjoyable part of their job is preparing pupils for life in a new multicultural Scotland. Having a worldview rooted in egalitarianism and victimhood, they are thusly in ideological lock-step with the ideas that underpin this agenda, such as White privilege and institutional racism. So that when such beliefs come up against inconvenient biological reality, then this reality has to be bent to their will. Such a response is not psychologically difficult if one believes that attainment gaps or failed multicultural ambitions are the result of institutional prejudice or a biased testing regime, if not outright discrimination. The school system, the teachers themselves and their institutional allies, will, then, do everything to deny or obscure disparate performance profiles and results, even up to the point of further scapegoating Whites for racial realities – for the ethnic-others must not be seen to fail! But humans cannot be other than what they are; this is a seventh level truth which can only be circumvented by a lie.

This has always been the end result of the multicultural project. The legal requirements and ideological commitment supersede educational goals and home culture norms, and so these must be altered to comply with the new reality to avoid 'victimising' ethnic-others by 'prejudicial' White standards. The circle is then squared by ensuring that everybody passes the new 'fairer' standards, all of which will be celebrated as a gain credited to multiculturalism.

The fact is our schools, like all our institutions, were built by us and exclusively for us, incorporating all the peculiar subtleties of philosophy and operation unique to us as a people; these features are of course as invisible to us, as they are natural to us. The efficient operation of these institutions is dependent on the smooth mesh of these human and institutional features; we do this easily. Others, however, less well. And the system can only incorporate these other peoples to the extent that they are compatible with this and wish to be. Often they are, but often they are not. They may still think they are, and we may want them to be, but the truth is accommodations have to be made. At first, and in a small way, this evolutionary adaptation may be useful, but eventually all these accommodations added together twist the institution out of shape to the point of inefficiency and then failure. Ultimately, there is no survival in a non-White educational world of White values and mores. We are now approaching this point; indeed, our policies and personnel are accelerating us to it.

Although responsible, the traitors and dupes within the education system are, in a sense, not to blame. Like Rachel's memory of her childhood in the movie *Bladerunner*, their belief has been planted, it feels true. This is what conditioning is. We will wait in vain for their *Aha!* moment and so we must proceed without this expectation.

Those teachers who have misgivings about all this, or even secretly disagree, are obliged to herd follow and take their badthink to private spaces. Integrity is compromised and the school divided into the Empire and the secret Rebel Alliance. Although, in a primary school, any secret is not so secret as there are more double agents in the staffroom than in a Bond movie. As a man, of course, any sympathetic rebel teacher one might meet will inevitably prove to be a Mata Hari.[25]

Western civilisation: bad; non-Western civilisation: good.

Our children's first contact with the institutions that govern and shape their life is in school, it should be a deeply ethical place, not a political one. However, the circumstances attendant upon the multicultural project make the avoidance of such politics impossible, as the system is stressed, then gamed, and high trust lost. High individual standards of ethics and morality are not compatible with this development and lead to the corruption of communal values.

By the time this current generation leaves school they will do so as emotional cripples, sheep-dipped in multicultural mantras, but largely ignorant of their antecedent's great achievements; worse, this pride-crushing absence is often replaced by the self-hate promoted by the continuous psy-ops projects of Hollywood, TV, UN and the MSM. You may not take pride in your ancestor's achievements, it hisses, as this history does not involve your personal contribution, but you can take blame and shame for supposed crimes committed by these same ancestors. Robbed of their ethnic prestige, but well-versed in the oppression narratives in which they as proxies occupy a central place, this false past becomes a mind weapon to steal the future. There is nothing sadder than self-hate and those so infected invariably respond in inchoate and then self-destructive ways.

The fundamental dishonesty of the multicultural school is killing our children spiritually, and leading them away from an ethical life by promoting the anti-social values it is apparently intended to combat. In this sense, then, schools have become like a cult camp requiring, as cults do, some daily act of obeisance. But, given to the wrong god, this surrender of our children's souls drains a little of their humanity. This is an attribute of multiculturalism that acts equally on all races! And it also reveals a truth about human nature: we don't feel a heartfelt belonging with racial outgroups, or to the social abstractions like the Aquarian vision of universal friendship and racial equality that underlie it. No matter how much we are told that we do – or we must do!

Who's doing this?

One could argue that the 'them' behind this replacement-level immigration, under the guise of multiculturalism as a moral imperative, is just the spirit of the times, and that this fever will run its course and break before we do; perhaps! However, the lessons from history are not optimistic about this. Many peoples and cultures have been extinguished, many of them once powerful and magnificent, but there are always reasons, and behind the reasons, hostile peoples. So too with us now! We agree with Nietzsche that whenever the spirit of the times is examined, it is revealed to be the spirit of the masters. And such masters that we now have do not love us, neither are they of us, nor our natural aristocrats. They are loyal only to themselves and their end-time vision. Using their control of the global platforms of thought and finance, they have initiated, led and funded movements, disingenuously named as democratic think-tanks or foundations for peace and justice, etc., which discredit the traditional foundations of Western society; Christianity, patriotism, our moral code, respect for the law, social homogeneity and sexual restraint. In every situation where they are present, even in small numbers, they are active on the side that will do harm to their native European host, and one would have to be completely obtuse to not notice this outsized tribal influence and the direction in which power flows. Once again, the warning from history, and the Bible, of never allowing this people positions of untrammelled power in your country heeded too late.

However, although Jewish activism has been a crucial part of this process, traditional Christian universalism and moral egalitarianism are also part of the equation. One could argue that Christianity carried the seeds of this destruction and, indeed, it continues to proselytise for the subversion of the West, while it also subverts itself. And too, we must credit the, previously mentioned, traitor-dupes and bought creatures, who willingly sell their souls for insider access (so they believe). This includes Western national governments who are, in certain crucial respects, just puppet fronts for the same agenda. And, considering the UK, and the dreck that passes for the highest offices of our country, can anyone doubt this? Now this 'spirit of the times', this mindfuck, turns its pitiless focus on our children.

With time, children can potentially recover from the pornification and inadvertent guilt-inducing intentions propagated by teacher-dupes, while possibly even forgiving them their weakness in fronting cultural misdirection as, referencing Jesus, they really didn't know what they were doing. However, our children cannot recover from not actually existing in that future. To be or not to be? – the future belongs to those who are present. And the strong preference from those who control the media platforms which shape our future world is for us not to be. To be as gone as, picking one from the genocide bucket list, Trojans are. This is conquest, but by demography, and our masters have their own reasons for wanting this which you will need discover for yourself. Real truths always have to be found, not told. Look to the matador, not the cape.

We Have Stepped In Too Far
To Turn Back

We were expected to accept and love other peoples, but separate from their virtues and their value to us. This was the starting position of the multicultural project; we could not be a judge to our own observations or feelings. However, it is realistically impossible to put others above our own self-interest, and it is also morally wrong. In uncritically elevating others, we do not demonstrate love or respect or kindness in action, but the supplicating and pathetic mindset of a slave before a tyrant master. By this power, Christian sacrifice was transformed into a call for racial suicide.

For the sake of our own children and our kind, we do not have the right to put the interests of others above them. Nor do we have the right to love others regardless of the consequences to our own. Such a love, unrequited as we daily see, is a pathology which has been forced on us. Indeed, everything about the multicultural project is forced, with lies piled on lies. But our fear of it has cowed us and all our responses demonstrate this fear. The hyperbolic attacks on the most innocuous of multicultural truth speakers (spewing hate, Nazi White supremacist, far right extremist, vile racist, rot in hell, etc.) by the media and social media are evidence of this.

The presence of massive numbers of disparate and otherly peoples is ultimately incompatible with our Western civilisation.

The final consequences of the multicultural programme will be played outside of school, but all are ultimately dependent on the indoctrination given while in school to undermine, enervate and enrage, respectively (according to ethnic group), and confuse and alienate all, irrespective.

This destruction of our hard won social capital and disrespect shown to our historic cultural genius occurs in front of children without them needing to understand it; the manipulations of results, the small-scale surrenders for an easy life, the affirmative action, the avoidance of topics, the harassing complaints, the wasted resources, the resource gaming, the secret resentments, the false celebrations, the loss of saying 'us' and 'we',[26] the fear of being doxxed as a racist; in short, the whole set of ideas linked to the other hatefuls. Ideas that just cannot be believed by thinking people, but still have to be accepted. This crisis with its endless exhortations and denouncements is exhausting for ordinary people. Further, it channels natural energies that should be spent on learning and fun into a negative dramatising of school life. In contrast to the enervated us and distracted others, the multicultural radicals are invigorated by the mayhem. Because as outsiders they feel no natural value or purpose to our social capital and cultural achievements, they would burn it as fuel on the revolutionary bonfire that celebrates the non-White future. Our children are just kindling to them.

The tragedy for us is that the crucial battleground of the primary school has been already lost to the multicultural forces, and that this will have to be recovered by men and female allies, mainly from forces outside of the schools themselves. This will be an attritional war, generations long, such is the embeddedness of the enemy in every institution connected with education.

Anti-racism is our future danger.

We Whites need to change ourselves from within to recover as a culture, even to survive as a distinct people. Our genetic inheritance,[27] specifics of history and Christian influence have rendered us uniquely vulnerable to appeals to victimhood and charity, and when these are combined with bad faith actors, we have a problem not solvable by our cultural naivety and reasonableness. Guilt and shaming tactics are crushing us between high and low-level predators and parasites. Tactics that do not work on differently constituted ethnic-others.

We stare agog at the anti-culture that rises before us.[28] And see that our intellects are now devoted to sustaining lies, yet still we can do nothing. Multiculturalism allied to political correctness in popular culture has already distorted production and reception of music, games, magazines, TV and movies, and our political system. In high culture, moralising authoritarians exert their severe influence into every corner. Creative and independent thought is corralled, cowed or destroyed.

We have been deeply foolish to have first permitted, and then enabled, the multiculturalism playing out in our society. It was a lie from the start and every solution to deny this reality became the driver of further collapse, leading us in turn to more lies and trickery. And creating in our schools the problem it apparently seeks to address. Ethnic-others, always more psychologically grounded in reality, know this better than us, although feel the turmoil just the same. Multiculturalism, then, essentially results in identity crisis for all in society. Diversity truly is a strength, but just not in any one country! Homogenous peoples want their own country, this is why different countries exist. Identity always trumps ideology and grandiose sentiments.

As we move from a democratic to a demographic age, to transition successfully we have to think of our own and break the conditioning that prevents us from talking about multiculturalism. For, if we do not control for biology, it will control us![29] It is not racist to be concerned about this. It is not demeaning of other peoples to do so.

The racism we hear lambasted was never a great evil in our country.

We deny our own the pride of ethnic prestige, but encourage the same in ethnic-others – how can this end well? Why should ethnic-others respect our cultural inheritance, and formerly safe communities, if we don't? We have been too willing to extend, without conditions, inclusion into our world as if it was of no value – why should we be surprised, then, if it is treated so? It should have been considered an honour to be permitted to belong to our community, instead of being a source of resentment. Hopefully, those ethnic-others will provide a necessary example of in-group self-interest and family focus, that being emulated may yet allow us Whites to rescue ourselves from the apocalypse unfolding before us. The time to take safety precautions is while still able to do so.

...and the answer to that initial question:

Not you anymore, you're too pale!

Summa Theologia Multiculturalismus

Tolerance, equality, inclusion and diversity, the principal ingredients of multiculturalism, are not virtues, but the infection vectors by which our schools will be transformed to propaganda factories. The resulting damage to our children's well-being is, at some level, willed. And behind this luring will is a motivating power that is evil. Moreover, it is not accidently evil as an unwanted, tragic outcome of other goals, the intention is deliberate. I have tried to resist anthropomorphising this force, but have come to the conclusion that not only is this the simplest way of expressing this intent, it is also the truest. Incompetence, indifference and ignorance also play a role, of course, but these are unconnected to the intent, being the normal features of an institution; their combined effect is to unwittingly divert us from the true intent that drives our fate. I have argued in this work for a conflation of different forces and factors coming together to create the situation our schools are in, however, when these are distilled to their essence, we are left with one power that rules them all. As always, in the end, there is only the one!

Under its banner of multiculturalism, psychological warfare is being conducted against us everywhere we look. But, the most important battleground in this war is in our schools; if we cannot protect our children from what is happening now, they will not be able to protect us from what is coming.

I do not believe we deserve this, but perhaps in that unknown realm where such decisions regarding our fate are made, deserved is nothing to do with it.

Omnes sancti orate pro nobis.

BREAKING

7
The UN

One Ring To Bind Them All

Introduction

Imagine you were full of hate for all peoples, although one more than any other as their achievements humiliated you, and they were ever your nemesis as you sought to make the world your own. Imagine you were also hubristic and, admittedly an unusual combination, had been hard-schooled in patience; so you can play the long game, to better enjoy your revenger dish cold. You decide that having your victims unwittingly destroy themselves would be the most satisfying experience; the pleasurable discord and confusion lasting generations would only end with their ending. At that time, too late for resistance, they would find out who led them to their fate. The plan, then? Easy; inspire the creation of a global organisation as a front for your agenda, staff it with your own in crucial positions, disguise this Golgotha of multicultural chaos by pretending it is a sort of big, happy, international café, whose self-anointed task is to rationally plan for a better world? Sometimes, of course, you would do good work, this is part of the gull; and it's fun seeing their enthusiasm in thinking that they are heading to a new beginning, when they are in fact marching into Sheol. Because people don't trust faceless organisations, give it a nice-sounding name and recruit some fancy pre-owned birds and well-known, useful idiots as glove puppets or pied pipers for the various deceits. We could call such united nations, the United Nations; for who could disagree with that? Even the abbreviation, UN, sounds good, although it is actually 'un'. The UN, all one needs to do is corrupt them. *Ha, ha!, only joking; that was already done at the get go!*

Satan is present here, in brightest form.
This is his time now.

The global project to remake mankind draws much of its legitimacy from the various UN pronouncements regarding social justice. Our schools too rely on this same authority to justify their inclusion of various future citizen goals that could be, or are otherwise, contentious. e.g., issues of racial justice, environmental activism, family structure and sexual politics, etc. Pupils, parents and staff are reminded of this authority by posters in school, charity initiatives and banners at the gates outside. Quietly building a UN brand loyalty while conferring its seigneurial favour on us, and just as quietly enforcing it; although it usually doesn't need to. After all, who wants to be seen as an opponent of *the ultimate* organisation dedicated to a better future for everyone, regardless of their origin, body form, birth race, birth gender, preferred pronoun and sexual preferences?[1]

WE ARE A UNICEF RIGHTS RESPECTING SCHOOL WHERE CHILDREN'S RIGHTS ARE LEARNED, UNDERSTOOD AND LIVED.

It must be wonderful to see this banner at the school gate every day; good old UN! Don't bother asking, though, what this specifically means, or why we need it, or how this goal is to be achieved. Don't bother asking how any of this is making your children's education better – there is no one to answer.

And especially don't bother asking just who authorised UNICEF, the UN's global social worker, to be the authority behind our children's rights. Just make sure that you patronise the UN approved Rainbow Alliance stall at the school fair and that your kid gets its face rainbow painted to support a new gender or homosexual choice in Uganda; a good thing to do at six years old.

Should one be curious,[2] though, and follow up this line of thinking, they will find that the UN produces its own justification via self-congratulation documents and videos in abundance; many smiling brown faces will be seen, but no evidence beyond the market-tested slogans. This is the sort of NLP mindwash, displayed in posters and banners at school that has a free ride into our children's minds. Thumped on the tom-tom every day, charity and rights. *You must!*

The thinking person knows that the UN's true role and its successes are much more ambiguous than its promo videos would have you believe, and that these are more in line with what you would expect in an organisation of such bureaucratic bloat and international skulduggery. In the long term, even the good works come to betray themselves. Indeed, much of its mission, properly viewed, was ever poorly fated; make-jobs, dodgy deals, 'white elephant' projects to loot state coffers, solving one problem to create another, pointless lists of endorsements and the like. Three generations in, the naïve intentions of its founding charter well debauched, the organisation is now a monster that exists for itself and its looters. Working with its partner (i.e., crony) organisations; the IMF, USAID, World Bank and WHO, the UN is best thought of as a vast international fence and launder operation for the multiple villainies of nature that swarm upon it; our oligarchic overlords and their nation-destroying banks, the dirty money tax shelters, the 'charitable' funds controlled by demonic philanthropists, the political leaders rotten with corruption, the shameless malfeasance of this vast circle of fraud. Often the UN achieves the opposite of the claimed intention, but still costs top dollar. But don't worry about paying for it, you already have! And in preparation for its receipt they've dug a money tunnel going all the way to Switzerland.

The Elders plunder us by running the West's capital through UN fronts in corrupted phony governments to end up back in their pockets. Properly viewed, even the corruption, incompetence and malfeasance is a misdirecting (although genuine) feature to

provide useful deniability; from the point of view of their agenda there is no true incompetence, but evil subtlety.

Such aspects of its operation are well-exposed elsewhere for those with an appetite for such fare.[3] We mention this here in passing to deny the UN its self-image as a presence for universal good and thus any special moral authority in our lives. Referencing contemporary social philosopher, Slavoj Zizek, so existentially false is it, that the UN is in actuality, its opposite, the un-UN!

The Globalist Agenda

But although the UN has become a byword for irrelevance, stupidity and a cesspit of venality, it is not without power.

And negative power, the power to hurt, is always the most persistent. The globalist agenda[4] currently being brought down on us like a sledgehammer throughout the entire world, has the UN as its Big Brother.

Imagine a world where everything is the opposite of a happy childhood; confusion and guilt circle like vultures, worldwide misery is brought to your eyeballs every day, and subversive degenerates are celebrated as a cultural norm, while the natural bonds of organic community are demonised. This is a war on the very conditions that make normal human society possible. All this takes place under the aegis of the UN.

This is what connects apparently disparate manifestations of our deep pathology: Third World funding tied to the adoption of progressive agendas by the recipient nations, lawfare against traditional organisations, entertainment hosting corrupting themes, charities that makes things worse, Bert and Ernie becoming gay on Sesame Street, the replacement population championed by banks,[5] the grants for self-hate projects,[6] the conflicting rights, etc., etc., and all leading us to: *A father in Texas has lost his legal battle to prevent his 7-year-old son from transitioning into a girl via chemical castration.*

Having now created the context we can now focus on our specific interest. And this is second and third order effects that spin off from the UN's family (i.e., European anti-family) propaganda branch, UNICEF, and its focus on the concepts of equality, justice, tolerance, child rights and the global citizens; ideas that are expressed as an ambition to reform the lot of children. And, further, to fix these changes in society by reforming the social and sexual attitudes of the children themselves. Western governments have taken these ideas and incorporated them into their school policies and curricula. As we have done in Scotland through the Curriculum for Excellence.[7]

To consider the effects of this agenda on our children, once again in this work we step beyond the direct cause and effect. Although this level of recursive thinking is alien to our everyday life, it is not a complex thing, merely requiring a little imagination added to experience of human nature, and some understanding of a child's worldview. This is the realm of the unseen, most of our internal life is lived there.

While it is easy to overstate these claims, it is even easier to understate. And underestimate!

These effects are that under the guise of its apparent universal authority, the UN claims and we unwittingly surrender to it, without actually doing anything, a part of our legitimate interest in our own children's welfare; this being their worldview, their attitudes to others and especially their exposure to philosophies relating to society, families and sexuality.

By right of blood, this interest should be exclusively ours. And normally it is jealously guarded against encroachment from deviancy; this is, after all, the job of being a parent. However, the apparent moral majesty of the UN's pronouncements, allied to its scale and reach, has a reassuring effect which serves to trick us to trust it and so bypass our natural defences. And, as the UN is faceless, costless at contact and its promulgations appear to have no immediate negative effect we ignore it. While it, allied with its progressive proxies, usually finding no organised resistance, establishes a new baseline for interference and ratchets forward further pronouncements on child education and welfare, always presented as extensions of human rights, racial justice and economic equality. These are then translated to law and public policy, as we have seen with our national curriculum, the Curriculum for Excellence; whose true focus, with its hubristic ambitions for global citizenship, peace, environmentalism, equity, racial justice and tolerance, is not academic, but political. This focus ultimately rests on the universalistic claims of UN charters and policy goals.

But, so what; it still seems so well-intentioned and, after all, 'it's for the children' – that irresistible coda that silences dissent – and who could object to that? Should you persist in your critical reflections, some might wonder, then, if you are one of those outmoded parents who do not respect children's rights, and would even 'go so far' as to deny them the free decision to choose their gender body form? [Cue *Booo!* from rent-a mob] And, if you are still harbouring doubts about the UN mission: *So you're in favour of African babies dying of thirst and children being beaten by their parents?*[8]

The danger to us parents lies in the fact that the ratcheting forward of UN inspired school-based justice policies and projects targeted at our children inevitably comes with sanctions against parents who object to this, even should they only partly do so, and only to the extent that it involves their own child. Suddenly, then, all those tiny incrementals, so kindly phrased, that you ignored, can now be seen as taking the ground from underneath you, and your right to your own child's mind and welfare. This control is now subject to others, who although they preached tolerance and a commitment to a shared vision, they did so to lull you. The shared vision did not include you. And already, too late, such tolerance is being wielded against 'haters', 'White supremacists' and 'recalcitrant parents' alike, although we know that the people called so are not such. This behaviour of progressive advocates is early-stage terrorism, but inside our heads.

Many of those influencing national policies on children are the foot-soldiers of the UN mission, formerly a fifth column, they now operate openly and 'with 'pride'-we have met them before in the other chapters.[9] Obsessed with identity politics, alienated from tradition and family, they are impatient for strong state intervention, with them at the helm, of course. Any disagreement with their objective, which they see as wholly benevolent, is anathematised; and the imposition of their vision, the UN vision, their master's vision, is then easily justified by appeals to the human rights, which they believe stands above and outside the democratic process, historical tradition and blood ties. These are the same people, who in previous times of discord, would crush you like an insect.

> **'Parents who disagree with the instructional materials related to gender, gender identity, gender expression and sexual orientation may not excuse their children from this instruction.'[10]**

Parental resistance then becomes the subject of legal scrutiny, and even police action – and police action is meant literally here, with officers removing children from their parents! And although such action is specific to the jurisdiction in which parents find themselves, they are ultimately sanctioned by reference to the UN diktats. This has already happened. And society's destructive elements, further emboldened, advance to the next level under the protective evil eye of their Big Brother UN. Perhaps we would have seen this coming if our MSM and political leaders had not been traitors and PR dollies for the same nation-destroying interests that lie behind the multicultural and sexual agenda.[11]

This situation, the threat of family focused tyranny by the state, is, then, where all this eventually leads; the denial of debate, the forcing of opinions onto your children, the accusations, the silencing and, as a locking cap, the hate speech laws. And the police down on you for something your kid may have inferred at school that could have hurt the feelings of a sensitive group or for 'making a racist facial expression'. We know that more of this turmoil is coming for us and our families and that some, the family-less, will welcome this. Goodwhites who believe they can fight this sort of thing by appeals to rational discourse and common decency have fatally underestimated their enemy, and are seriously outgunned. Such claims as ours here are often described as hyperbolic and inevitably become dismissed as conspiracy theories. However, when one steps aside from MSM sources and critically examines the situation they find there is indeed a conspiracy, but one to keep the sheer madness of this evil beclownment of our world from public knowledge.

Human Rights and Wrongs

Human rights are used as a justification for legislation
to destroy the opposition. The hate groups that
they identify are not hate groups, but hate targets.
And there is only one true target.[12]

The true target of the UN human rights agenda is ethnic Whites.
They alone among the races are susceptible to universalistic moral
appeals, for ethnic-others more properly locate their social concern
to their own ethnicity, tribe or even family. Whites alone apparently
must learn to 'embrace diversity' and 'challenge stereotypes.' But
here they come to learn that such ideas are not advanced in a
general sense, but rather as part of an interlocking set designed to
evoke all of the social justice ambitions than define the UN mission
to us. And by this, planting deep in our children's minds the idea that
remedies must be undertaken by us Whites, who are tacitly assumed
responsible for all this apparent injustice, via our alleged racism and
sexism.[13] The intent of this is to create guilt, and by this ensure a
steady supply of compassion to fund the endless obligations to the
ethnic-others, who are supposedly always so needful. In this eternal
crusade of subliminal begging advertisements, enough is never
enough. Power is taken away from us in exchange for responsibility
to others; others, our children hard learn, whose own habits and
culpability in their predicament can never be questioned; and
likewise, the hostile global cabal who control our world. The bottom
line is always the same message; this is better known as mind
programming. This is the tragedy being built into our children's lives.

These beliefs, and the related legitimacy of the UN as promotor and guarantor, are cemented among the impressionable young by the recruitment of spiritual vampires like Bono and teeny-brained poptarts[14] and actors as UN 'special ambassadors' for multicultural kindness or sexual tolerance. For if it was not for the familiar pouting faces of these idiot-traitors personalising the message, people could more easily appreciate the faceless bureaucracy that lies behind the agenda, and perhaps even the snake-philanthropists behind that.

Such creed may look human like us, but the spirit of these totally owned creatures who stand before our children is totally contrary to us. A better idea of their true nature would be obtained by thinking of them as narcissist apparatchiks within the entertainment division of Globohomo Futureworld; in short, propaganda tools. They do what they are told. And, as professional entertainers, are able to act out the caring or empowered role as required.[15] Of course they care too, but in a special way that draws favourable and sexy attention to themselves from the media that owns them, just as they would for a modelling assignment or a new product promo. Such public faces run the UN mission no risk, as they are only able to speak in slogans and so can never go rogue. And they assuredly provide a friendlier face in comparison to some real-life alternative UNESCO poster children – a 40-year-old (she wishes) drag queen, trans-vamp 'educator', or a cannibal warlord from Liberia.[16] Here we demonstrate the truth of the claim that propaganda is all about optics; for if what the UN was promoting was honest and true, it would not need to be propagandised so relentlessly, and by such famous celebrities.

As if what the Western world really needs are more feminist activists and carbon deficit celebrities to save the planet by jetting around it! As if who needs mothers and fathers as role models for children, when you can have UN ambassadors championing adopting Third World orphans – even if only by the proxy of global charities? And, not having children of their own, how psychologically easy and personally consoling it must be to them to brainwash young White females into barrenness in order to save the planet from over-population. If they could, they would take a giant chainsaw to the White demographic and call it justice. This cynical reading of Tikkun Olam, supposedly healing the world by destroying us Whites, is not hard to find in the mainstream media, and is hard to *not* find on social media.[17]

Our children are helpless in the face of such an offensive involving their heroes and role models, for they cannot understand the action of diabolical narcissism, nor begin to conceive of the extent of their manipulation and the complicit acquiescence by their teachers. Nor, hearing these role models spewing their bog-standard rhetoric of victimhood, minority worship and female empowerment, can they realise how profoundly vacant and conformist most of these star ambassadors actually are.

How cheap it is for these special ambassadors to assuage their creeping guilt by virtue signalling while self-promoting on the UN's account. But, fear naught for justice, for theirs really is a Mephistophelean bargain; selling their people and their soul for a few years headlining in the puppet booth against an eternity of *the reckoning.*

Sowing the Bad Seed

Under the UN flag:
anti-male, anti-feminine, anti-White,
anti-family, anti-freedom propaganda.

The UNICEF flag flies at the school gate ever reminding the child (and parent) of social justice and their well-learned guilt; and prepping the future mind for future 'equalisations' and new norms at home and abroad

In our children's minds, such flags and banners play a subtle, visual role, in conjunction with buzz words like 'humanitarian' or 'democracy' or 'crisis', to help legitimise the concept of Western political and military intervention in other countries, as well as obviously by direct UN intervention itself. It is surely not contentious to regard some of these interventions as manipulative of these fundamental principles, and to posit that, at least, part of the apathy and surrender of Western public opinion to such actions is due to this early training.

Thusly, have our schools become political places.

UNICEF is also a part of the process that legitimises the creation of a protester mindset among our children which further alienates them from their home culture. In concert with the other forces examined in this work, it does this by implication; native White culture being presented as essentially prejudiced, misinformed and otherwise unfair and requiring to be challenged by hero-children.[18] This protester mindset can express itself in many different, even contradictory, ways. (e.g., protesting at government intervention, protesting at no government intervention, protesting mega-corporations while funded by them). Such contradictions, though, are irrelevant as far as the principle of youth protest is concerned; whatever position is adopted or action taken (or not) still justifies the protest and the notion of youth power as a popular lever for particular government actions. It is by this means that further state intervention is legitimised; for here it can present itself as responding to popular demand. This development, then, is not to be welcomed as an extension of democracy. For the children so activated, in fact, represent the opposite of this, and the ultimate in remote control. It is literally child's play to manipulate this impressionable cohort, via MSM, social media and youthful crisis actors, into protesting a pre-chosen issue and then to represent the protests as spontaneous. This is the practice known as 'manufacturing consent', which wise men have always drawn concerned attention to; such Jeremiahs, however, never expected this process to target younger children. For the primary school pupil, this direct activation is only a little into their future; however, the preparation for the 'correct' mindset can never start too early.[19]

This protester tendency is especially damaging of girls who are evidently more susceptible to feminist and globalist group-think propaganda. The feminist rebels and 'bad girls saving the world by doing men things better than men' is an irresistible trope, endlessly repeated in female/teen magazines, blogs and on screen; it is inevitable that young girls would wish to emulate this. And it was inevitable too that this would be manipulated; and probably no creature is easier to manipulate by such tropes and appeals as the female teen. It is not an accident, then, that protester movements typically involve large herds of girls, chaperoned (ironically) by overweight fem-witches and ancient barren banshees, many of whom were once young and slimmer, but equally as empowered and self-righteous as their youthful co-protesters.[20] Such a protester mindset may be futile, but it is certainly not without power to harm;

and a proportion of such girls evolve to womanhood with their heads still full of this worrisome burden whose end effect for them is anti-family and ultimately anti-life. This is divide and conquer tactics, the girls so activated tragically unaware that they are dividing and conquering themselves. The tales of such women who, alas too late, come to see how their lives have been led to emptiness make tragic and instructive reading. Would it be that these examples were told in place of kick-ass termagants!

More generally, though, this protester conscience can also make all children enemies of themselves by encouraging morbid thoughts on issues which they do not well understand, cannot effectively combat and so render themselves ripe for further manipulation – and depression. Witness the tragic Greta T as a present and future example of these wounded birds, born of anxiousness.

UNICEF's benediction can be likened to a psy-op to create little Manchurian candidates for the global multicultural and multi-sexual reorientation of the West.

As the UN and powerful celebs authorise, justify and even sanctify such activism, this further encourages the creation of a self-righteousness that is not becoming in a youngster; this in turn inevitably becomes judgemental, even condemnatory. Such powerful forces in a young mind risk pathologising the personality, and the innocence proper to their lives at this stage may never be recovered. This is not to say that the young mind should avoid reality and only be concerned with puppies and rainbows, however, this issue is altered when political activism is encouraged. This early introduction to politicised topics and activism never ends well for those so infected. In the short term, the dopamine addicted child gods who berate and demand; while over the longer term, it leads to the development of a negative view of future life which darkly shades the young person's view of their own future. Schools should not be party to allowing such manipulation under the UN banner.

In like manner, UNICEF contributes to the alienation of children from their parents. This is a background effect, of course, subtly achieved through the agency of all the major subversive influences which seek to influence their worldview, their priorities and the legitimisation of the attitudes which flow from this. To empower children this way, intentionally and independently of their parent's authority, is to disempower adults generally and parents in particular. Growing children hardly need more encouragement to believe in their infallibility and their right to enjoy whatever they have been encouraged to believe is their rights.

The tolerance and rights espoused by UN ordinances do not add anything to the responsibility that parents should have for their own children, and us Europeans especially don't need them. Most of us operate by our own inbuilt coding, evolved over aeons to ensure that the society we have created for our families continues to provide the values and security our families need. Where this has failed is, as often as not, due to thse very same forces of tolerance and faux compassion, which undermined the traditional family and led us to the situation we are now in. Those families which do need such rights expounded and enforced are our collective responsibility, but only in our own society. Others from other places must look to their own traditions, this is their prerogative and their responsibility; and we need to let them, free from officious, patronising and corrupting Western influence.

Rejecting the Golem

Tolerance, equality, charity, justice, freedom, equity, diversity and human rights, the whole UN package, are not the goals so much as the infection vectors into our schools.

When you support them or silently acquiesce, you support the normalisation of deviance and complaint, guilt and entitlement; and, in time, the compete convergence of our schools into propaganda factories for the destruction of the West. All the grand and uplifting themes of Western civilisation have been hijacked and replaced by power relations between groups. This view is crude, ungrateful and a lie.

Properly viewed, and future extrapolating in a loving concern for our children's welfare, I believe that the UN's interference is an evil force in our schools. Naturally, they present themselves as the doorway through which the world will find justice and rationality in our new nationless, rainbow regions. But for us Whites the door is a trapdoor to the world's basement. Us, the trapped givers; the others, ever indigent. Us, ever guilty; them, ever entitled. This is a process that is focused inexorably on producing doom; and at the end of this process – the raceless, nationless, multi-sex monoculture at the end of history. Raceless meaning ours; everyone else's will be well represented. And celebrated!

We, and especially our children, are being subject to a disempowerment project posing as an empowerment project. And everything argued for in this chapter is part of this plan, which is interlocking with other elements discussed in earlier chapters, to create a moral obligation to Westerners, but increasingly backed by the relentless application of the law. There is almost nothing holding these forces back, now that they have their justification, authority, funding and sigil in the UN; the ring to bind them all.

Almost nothing holding them back, but us.

Call To Arms

Good parents look behind the multiplicity of political catchwords and well-intentioned claims fronted by false-faced ambassadors to see UNICEF for what it is; a front to legitimise the propagandising of your child and a guilt distribution service operated as if a franchise. See how they will use your child's rights as a hammer to crush you, should you resist. Our children are becoming increasingly captive to events set in motion within our primary schools. The time to take safety precautions is now. It has to be sooner, there won't be a later.

THE MISGUIDED EIGHTH

8
Women Teachers

Free At Last

Women Teachers

Just As Well It's Not a Man Doing the Criticising

In this work we have referred to the many interconnected reasons that have led our schools to their present situation. There is, however, one crucial factor that we have not referred to with enough emphasis and that is the overwhelming presence of women in primary teaching.[1] This is important because many, possibly most, of them are in fundamental agreement with the tenets of the harmful seven for reason particular to their psychology and their current position in Western society, at least as they see it. This happy concordance between the harmful seven agenda and the widely embraced feminist assumptions of the profession, result in a failure to critically consider this agenda as well as a certain zealotry in deliverance that would otherwise be absent.

Indeed, it could be argued that feminist brainwash is *the* crucial factor that enables the harmful seven, as these will not just appeal to women by their nature, but be viewed as imperatives in the same female struggle against the patriarchy,[2] male imperialism and toxic masculinity; the whole UN designer handbag of eco-no gender-green-victim-anti-whatever continuously pumped into this generation of females by every means available. It is not accidental then that certain features of the harmful seven are often expressed as an aspect of global female empowerment and female justice. That women can virtue signal about this too nicely ties up the whole sell.

Considering this further, we note that the essentially conformist nature of women, ever seeking group acceptance, both with respect to each other (in public) and to the dominant ideology, result in a compact that will prevail up to the point of destruction.[3] Also, female career advancement in schools is so much more dependent on embracing this orthodoxy that few risk transgressions against it. Thusly and hence, women beware women. The few men in such female systems have to accommodate to this female reality which continually works to filter out any masculine impulse towards observable physical reality that might threaten the narrative. Any man expressing scepticism would be easily out-grouped as heartless and some variant of –ist, and then destroyed. Indeed, it is in the stomping of a low status male with the wrong opinions, such as a male primary school teacher, that otherwise divided female teachers would find their sisterhood[4] in this bacchanal.[5]

Western women, and especially the more intelligent and further educated, are powerless to resist this gigantic cultural con, which has exploited their innate qualities as caregivers[6] by linking this to the wider political goals discussed in this work. Exceptions excepted, the strong maternal instincts and organisational genius of women finds its best expression in small-scale, family or community activity; hence the many great female primary teachers. Scaled up to societal level, however, these same instincts, when turned into public policy, eventually prove to be divisive and socially damaging. Hence the concept of 'pathological altruism' as the natural tendency of female dominated Western societies, a phenomenon that is compounded in female dominated institutions, such as our primary schools. The harmful seven are perhaps the ultimate expression of this.

And it is in this situation, faced with the harmful seven and witnessing their consequences, that the female's innate weaknesses come into play: Firstly, that of future-vision, or rather, lack of; inevitably resulting in a failure to appreciate the long-term societal consequences of this scaling-up of virtue signalling, meddlesome nannying and herd-think. Then, later, the obstinate refusal to accept the evidence and admit error; and instead double down and transfer blame. This especially applies to female managers, who, generally being inherently indifferent to the notion of honour, have no ethical problem following any orders, or offloading costs and risks to inferiors; hence, the existential crisis in primary schools is unfixable. In such a situation, men vacate and leave women to their own devices. This is the hard tragedy that looms ahead for our school system and into which the girls rush with self-righteous madness. Tweeting LOL!

So the pretty lies of progress obscure the ruthlessness of trading kindly future hopes against hard-hearted (but clear-visioned) nature. It is a tragedy for us all that our culture fails to provide any sort of feminine guidance to young women, starting at home and in primary school. This tractoring of the female mindset is central to the harmful seven. The cat ladies, angry fembots and vast majority of well-meaning, misguided eighth are mass produced like this from the factory, already defective and earmarked for extinction – yours and ours.

Opposition to the harmful seven will then have to come from outside the school system, and to the extent that male men are involved in this, we can expect a proportionate indignant reaction.

If this belief-chain terminates anywhere, it is where the howling is.

Addendum

By way of defence against certain claims, but without apology. Sorry, Girls, not sorry!

Never Apologise

The best of creatures
our better halves
mother nurse wife country
fertile soil of all our
dreams and ambitions
from flights of fancy

to ploughed soil of our
future champions
not friend but better
or worse and all in hope
that women will love us
as we love them.

Notes

1: Tolerance

1   Which was not tolerated. So intolerant was the system to tolerance that perhaps it seems a minor miracle to modern readers that children ended the school day alive and well.

2   Svart hål; it sounds better in Swedish. Or even better, röv!

3   Hereafter, I assume that the reader understands now my particular and sneering use of the term. Same for 'our values'.

4   This is a common occurrence with educational practice and educational psychology. Such is the tautological nature and basic meaningless of so many of the core concepts that one finds that concepts and definitions can be swapped around with no loss (or increase) in meaning. e.g., learning skills, targets and outcomes and SEAL maths are good (in the bad sense) examples of this effect. Indeed, SEAL may be the *Finnegans Wake* of recovery maths. A certain grim fun is to be had in playfully swapping definitions around and seeing if anyone notices; although they don't. One may laugh, but scammers get paid more than you for writing this demoralising nonsense.

5   Good pronoun awareness! *Thank you for noticing.*

6   As it always is! A suspicious person might even think that lawyers and suchlike creed are behind such initiatives.

7   Check the Curriculum for Excellence capacities section; confused learners, entitled individuals, disruptive citizens, negative contributors. Incidentally, it is fitting that a curriculum document that has sown such discord with its every pronouncement should find this meaningless fungibility in its mission statement. This fun cost us millions to produce.

8   Asking the same to the class teacher may be a thing to do for giggles, but no more enlightening than asking a puppy. And you would be denied the possibility of breaking the tension by throwing a stick.

9   I have never heard, or heard of, a management person of any grade, far less seniors, explain or justify the values content of the curriculum.

10   I find myself entertaining two simultaneous thoughts at such presentations. Firstly, embarrassed for the presenters, so stupid are they. Secondly, as such women (as they always are) are generally lippy, self-satisfied activist types, exactly who the branks were made for, in a little reverie I see myself enforcing the wise city laws of our forefathers – to rapturous applause of the female audience.

11   You don't need a medical degree to use this; it's just an infographic sheet. In attempting to generate sympathy for the predicament of transgender people, the information contained in the' toolkit' emphasising the strikingly high levels of health and mental health problems suffered by such individuals, ends up unwittingly providing a counter-argument to its own thesis. The use of the word 'toolkit', like 'workshop' (A toolkit will be issued at the workshop) is typical of the hyperbolic nonsense language which has replaced English in educational circles. It is, of course, unnecessary to attempt to generate sympathy for such people; almost everyone has sympathy for their predicament. And perhaps, even especially so, among those concerned about the social consequences of this activism. It is clear that this is a project that is being driven by powerful interests within and behind the media, and not necessarily by the trannies themselves; excepting the narcissists among them.

12   The lawsuits have already arrived in the US, typically facilitated (and funded) by the same interests that promoted the policy changes. As these developments are common to the Western World, so too will we in far-flung Scotland eventually find ourselves in Discordia. California, here we come!

13   I believe that an unconsidered aspect of the early introduction of gender politics into schools is to alter how boys and girls think of each other, shifting their natural competition from the biological to the political sphere. Thus deeply planted, this returns in teenage and early adult life as a compromising force in the forming of lasting love and family prospects.

14   It's a vulgar word to describe a parent's treatment of their child, but accurate.

15   Epictetus: *Look not for any greater harm than this: destroying the trustworthy, self-respecting, well-behaved man within you.* It is a lynchpin of Stoic thought that the thing that brings down a man is shame.

16   Parents are correct in their instincts, as this demographic is always over-represented in child molestation incidents.

17 That's why George and Freddie are no longer with us, Michael and Mercury respectively or, as this is a factual work, Panayiotou and Bulsara.

18 But never so activist as to waive their fees; well, lawyers have to eat and drink like the rest of us, but just a bit better!

19 Perhaps this seems as an unwarranted heavy judgement: However, based on direct observation, it seems to me that many in this group lead the life of witches and live on the periphery of social life as outcasts. Here they procreate, not by having babies, but by imposing their ideology on other people's children. Having rejected natural goodness their spirits become spiteful and, by the necessary consequence of this, find themselves compelled to destroy the most beautiful of that which they cannot have, our children and thereby our future. Their subhuman bodies, mutilating enhancements and sheared haircuts are often a giveaway.

20 Fun Fact: This was originally auto-completed to pubic faces, which makes a certain sense too.

21 e.g., The trans women group (Femen) funding. They suddenly found out who owned their voice when they targeted the wrong country (guess which; just joking, I know you know!) for action.

22 e.g., Mary Whitehouse. In her case it's late in coming, but now heartfelt, and so; respect. She was basically right, and I was basically wrong. She had a nude magazine mockingly named after her by porn publishing, demon-king David Sullivan which, properly considered, is a very fulsome tribute.

23 Proverbs; 17:22 *A merry heart doeth good like a medicine: but a broken spirit drieth the bones.*

24 Misogyny alert: brotherhood here has the audacity to incorporate sisterhood, xyzterhood, etc., etc.

25 Keep reaching for that rainbow and keep taking that Lupron.

26 But actually is JCVD. He's not gay and he's not pleased to see you; it really is a gun. These White bigot guys never seem to see that the stranger ordering a glass of milk looks like he is made of concrete, with a chest like an Aga stove under his well-worn, French Foreign Legion combat shirt.

2: Anti-bullying

1   The evidence for the efficacy of such programmes is never asked for or presented. It would be instructive to have expenditure and outcome tracked, and then publicly presented, for the thousands of such Utopian initiatives implemented in the last fifty years. It would be even better to have their named champions held accountable; instead, as burglars, they disappear into the night with the loot.

2   American pupil, in America, hence ass. This dates from the Ninja Turtles era. Imagine, if you can, the accompanying artwork; it was hilarious. And, although easily the strongest message (DON'T BULLY-OR THE NINJA TURTLES WILL KICK YOUR BUTT), it unfortunately was not selected for the school Anti-bully Week poster.

3   It is, of course, fashionable to pretend that such pupils do not exist. In a school setting such pretence is a condition of continued employment. Some of the euphemisms used to describe such pupils are unintentionally comic; alternative processing, instruction resistant, adopts non-compliance strategies, task averse, work completion insecurity, etc. With such absurd denial woven into the fabric of education, the writing of Franz Kafka recommends itself for compare and contrast.

4   Only one of this list is bogus and, although this example is frankly unlikely, it nicely illustrates what would be regarded as a traditional bullying incident. *And, by the way, you're smelly and eat worms, and everybody hates you!*

5   With respect to the issue of protecting vulnerable children we, and our children via MSM, have witnessed a series of spectacular, generation-long failures. This is, of course, not discussed in schools, but the knowledge is there and by upper primary children begin to understand in wordless form the connection between this societal betrayal of children by high talk and low action, and the same in school with bullying; and especially so should there be a racial element. Generally speaking, a non-White child could persecute a White child with near impunity, the opposite (even if just inferred) would draw down the majesty of the law (and school policy) to the last syllable and frown. Children see this happening, and their innate sense of justice cannot but be harmed by this, and then carried to the future to manifest in some negative way.

6   However, in this age of ours, where kindness and tolerance are enforced with an iron rod, one has to wonder who exactly are the bullies now? Certainly,

as a tempting target, nothing can beat the class teacher. For here, callous management, tell-tale pupils and idiot-tweeter parents can form a happy triumvirate of torment while gaming the system, which bends over backwards to accommodate them. For the sociopaths involved, it presumably feels transcendental to freely persecute and feel righteous for doing so. This is their little heaven on Earth.

7   It is not accidental that this is the most common trope of our self-discovery stories and especially when they are made into movies. It is in this act of standing up for yourself, that one's essential self is revealed. This power must be allowed its space, both psychological and social, to exist. A male's well-being depends on its presence. The anti-bully programmes compromise the discovery of this. Denied this knowledge, one can be made harmless. This is not a virtue in the male world, nor regarded so by females; thus explaining, incidentally, the female's otherwise perplexing advocacy of (when immigrants), and general attraction to, violent males.

8   It will be interesting to see how the upcoming generation ages into adulthood with many having had little to no experience of a respectable male authority figure in their formative years, whether in primary school or even in their home life. The corrective to this absence that youth organisations may have provided in the past having also been removed by IT life and lawfare.

9   This is not picking on females, but just recognising that their natural solipsism generally prevents any awareness of the long-term consequences of such behaviour and any self-awareness of hypocrisy when silencing anyone who questions their viewpoint. It also appeals to their permanent palace conspiracy mindset. This all done beneath the male radar, such stealth flying being like autopilot to most females; as many men eventually discover following their appointment with the law court:

...fortunately a member of the public visiting the pub recorded his sexist remarks on camera, contacted the police and was able to provide evidence to the authorities. Following a viral campaign, Mr White has been permanently relieved of his duties. His former employer stated that...

Half the country's women, it seems, are would-be Stasi officers on patrol for bad-think men. Obviously, this is a good thing; it's not right that a group of men could privately get together and make disparaging remarks or jokes about females. The walls (well, Big Sister's smart phone) have ears!

10   Under such a teacher, and the many like him, victimhood culture would have been strangled at birth. The final passing of such based teachers (male and female) by about 1990 was a necessary condition for the safe arrival of the current politicised, activist agenda; this being just one aspect of the terrible, planned concinnity that led our schools to their current predicament. One wonders whether such old school teaching values could make a return if given a stylish make-over and new tag; e.g., Neo-brutalism, Shock Force 10, Nu-Victorian Overseer, etc.

It is interesting how one's understanding changes over 50 years. I never thought that I would ever pass a favourable remark on Mr Reid's robust and overly-masculine teaching style, but I can now see a certain utility to it; and I did learn to use a slide rule. So, thanks for that. However, this is not remembering fondly.

11   I wonder too if the retreat of males from much of public life, and too of institutions dominated by women (like primary teaching) in some convoluted way refers back to a boy's first experience of the feminine mode of resolving grievances like in anti-bully programmes, and a well-founded fear of this allied to a feminist viewpoint and agenda. As an example I have noticed that such childhood equivalents, for example anti-bully clubs, are dominated by articulate and super-confident little girls; what boy would want to be part of this? As a man, and for the want of a quiet life, one instinctively turns away from such bodies. I wonder if the anti-bully programmes and victimhood culture comes to be understood by boys as a first indication of how female agendas will dominate female dominated workplaces. Such are an early indication of how the world is to be, and it's not a man's world. James Brown's great song was from 50 years ago; of which, see James and Luciano's charity concert from 2002 on Youtube.

12   It is entertaining to consider the nature of a teacher's visit to the HT's office following a pupil actioning this advice: *Did you tell pupil X to punch pupil Y on the face? The police are very interested in your answer.* (Names replaced for anonymity. X being Brandon, Y being Leon)

We have also been informed that you replaced the anti-bully restorative workshop lessons with exerts from the Jean Claude van Damme movie, Kickboxer, claiming it provided better anti-bullying advice. Is this true?

The answer to both questions is yes.

13   See William Wallace at Lambhill Street School (in The Belt Room) for a nice example of the operation of this principle.

14   It is instructive in this regard to consider how some of the world's most notorious bullies, certain lawsuit-slappy billionaire tycoons spring to mind, adopted the protective mantle of the eternal victim, endlessly bullied for his ethnicity. But not, apparently, for his personal conduct or business practices.

15   That moment – the ultimate in performance art – when *To be or not to be* becomes a hard reality. And one finds whether:

> *'tis nobler in the mind to suffer*
> *The slings and arrows of outrageous fortune,*
> *Or to take Arms against a Sea of troubles,*
> *And by opposing end them.*

16   Don't worry if you don't take them, they leach into groundwater supplies. Ask big pharma about this; I'm sure they will fund a study into this – on the day that hell freezes over!

3: Charity

1   Thinks: *Husbandless, large families?* If only life was that simple, the African mother would have a husband and her dowry would be a herd of goats.

2   See Jesus' parable of the widow's mite.

3   By wealth, I am here referring here to the various extra financial costs, in addition to what you may directly give. These are especially associated with Third World and global charity initiatives and are invisibly levied and similarly spent through unravellable government channels. This comes to untold billions flushed to oblivion; well, actually, Swiss accounts. Such costs are not even limited to direct giver-receiver lines, but backwend (as a sort of evil interest finally returned) to the host with extra costs and policy obligations resulting. The refugee industry could arguably be considered as one such topical example

4   Charity, just another weapon in the narcissist's arsenal.

5   An example, arguably not evil, of how misdirected and dyscivic such impulses can become when decoupled, is the sex cam-hoor offering access to

increasingly intimate views of her own koala by the increasing dollar donation to the charity that rescues Australian fire victim koalas – so she claims (as I was told). Sex, money and victims, the triple unlocked!

6   Arguably this badge collecting is the point of the whole exercise, like a virtuous form of stamp collecting (male HT) or posting online pictures of their shoes (female HT) or rainbow rallies attended (other gendered HT).

7   One soft toy had a large HIGHLY FLAMMABLE label attached. Considering the destination, it seemed like sending a hand grenade. To be fair, some gift boxes were very considerately completed; however, this is no guarantee of their suitability to the receiving child.

8   In the interests of anonymity, not her real name; which is Emmie.

9   She demonstrated a virtue of honesty which I felt more than compensated for her strategic forgetfulness. *Just sweeties*, when asked how the money was spent. This child simultaneously demonstrated good BS detectors, a proper sense of infant priorities and a strong survival instinct. All good!

10   It's not really Western, it's the *them* that puppet master our Western governments. Westerners just do the deeds of destruction, get the blame and pay the price. And not least, the psychic, spiritual and (who knows?) eternal one!

11   This claim may seem excessively conspiratorial for a societal trend managed through bureaucracies; however, ultimately this trend is an expression of the strong approval – if not the will – of certain people whose values, scope and pathologies find this this development congenial. This is the curtain behind the curtain.

12   I've had the question asked by a 6 year old. And what a question! *Answer that, Solomon!*

13   Lest the children forget to otherwise top up on their daily dose of guilt, these signs pinned to a classroom (P3) door with the exhortation: *How can we make a difference?*

     Pure propaganda. And all this mandated by our most excellently virtuous Curriculum of Excellence. *Hail!,Hail!, to the ineffable (and ef-able!) goodness of its architects and the wisdom of our leaders in promoting it. May they get charity back in true proportion to their giving.*

I am truly sorry for the African farmer, the child who drinks dirty water and little Meera. I wish them well in finding a way to fix their own problems. And I am grateful for my ancestors' efforts and sacrifices that led to my privilege.

14   Wilberforce at 6000 rpm! This week' assembly focus is to leverage funds to help stamp out slavery in Africa. Pilton and the Hebrides ignored again!

4: BBC *Newsround*

1   In actuality it is only apparently indispensable. In real life it is dispensable and after the departure of withdrawal symptoms, whole new vistas open up and TV news can be more clearly seen for what it is; anathema. The false creatures who front it then become unwatchable. And that's you cured! With respect to TV, you know what you are missing; with respect to no TV, you don't know what you are missing. So far, you can exercise this free will without restriction, although your media owners will know via your smart TV that you are thinking outside the box. Currently, they will just offer you a better package. In the future you will be questioned under arrest.

2   Although it is and I am.

3   This raises an interesting point about the role of teachers in this process of brainwashing; are they puppets or useful idiots. The difference, admittedly subtle, being that the puppet does not know they are being used, whereas the useful idiot willingly contributes to a project, mistakenly (stupidly) believing that they are a respected contributor to a worthy cause. Undoubtedly, both types are well-represented – sometimes in the same person! I'm giving teachers the benefit of the doubt that they incline more to puppets. It should be noted that this remark is not made as a kindly gesture to female sensitivity, but in recognition of lesser agency; it being the contention that most women teachers are not inclined, or otherwise able, to find the level of recursiveness required to reveal their true complicity. Except for me and another guy, this holds true for male teachers too.

4   See the named person scheme which was roundly condemned as anti-democratic and against the laws of nature, even by Kim Jong-un and Boko Haram. Among the named persons could be a traffic warden, local LGBT+ coordinator or Uber driver. It goes without saying that your priest, imam or rabbi would be popular candidates for such a task,...with themselves.

5   Except obloquy for your own observations, whatever they may be, regarding race, intelligence, predilection for crime, corruption, sexual degeneracy, funding of NGOs and the presence of tribal-merchants as the ghost in the machine.

6   That was me. I was attempting to develop my global presence to sell books and other branded items.

7   Drop the idol worship. They are clickbait for product placements and wrong lifestyles. Why do so many little girls end up dressing like plastic celeb skanks and posting prurient nonsense (or worse) online, think ye?

8   There are advocates for children being exposed to, and then encouraged to discuss, news. As an example of a pro news extremist, see Picture News. Here they state that 'child-friendly news is important because it makes information accessible and encourages children to think critically about events and key issues.' No argument is developed, nor evidence presented, in making this assertion. Their entire thesis is a list of cut and paste globalist social justice clichés ; challenging perceptions', 'being empowered', 'making a difference', 'relate and empathise', all of which is intended to help children realise that 'they too can change things and make a difference.' You can easily imagine what differences are intended when a stated goal is to get children to 'relate and empathise with people in circumstances very different to their own.' (But not, for example, home-based, girl victims of rape gangs.) With its unexamined assumptions, evidence-less hope and a total lack of awareness of how compromised by its corporate owners the news is, this website is the very epitome of a useful idiot shading into evil angel. There is no sense here of any negative consequences – even while ironically advocating 'keeping calm' and being a good 'emotional role model' – when children are exposed to disturbing news. It is interesting to speculate if such superficial thinking as this is more evidence of the forward march of morons with an eye to shaking down a couple of shekels, or this is a part of some intel psy ops against our children. Certainly, if I was a certain news platform owner interested in destroying the psychic welfare of other people's children, I would transfer 30 pieces of silver to such a sock puppet for their kind advocacy of my brand and world view. I already own their soul.

9   e.g., Lewis Hamilton vegan burgers, the girl band who are rescuing monkeys, Brit Award hopefuls, the Zulu boy making carbon friendly shoes from tofu, super new homework app-see BBC Future for more details, etc.

10   I've got a thing about youth ambassadors-no, not *that* sort of thing; but *this* sort of thing that sees their narcissism, shallowness and stupidity combining to willingly sell their souls. They believe, as they have to, that their fictional ambassador role somehow assuages their soul-deep sense of worthlessness, when in fact it compounds it. The proper payback comes later. I pity them as I hate what they do. Satan never bought so cheaply as when he made a wholesale deal with the UN.

The idea of globo Chucky doll Greta T scolding the world on carbon usage, or millionairess Emma W lipsyncing on the patriarchy blocking female achievement and objectifying women while being snapped half naked is [select preferred outrage emoji]. However, on the positive side; thank you to Emma for not having children of her own to fly to Florida for a Disneyland holiday. That's saved some carbon points for India to be traded against Emma's top dollar Mercedes sports cabriolet. (*It's ok, as an independent woman she doesn't have to apologise for it.*). Grrr!

11   The desire for knowledge of how to control opinions by such means is why this research was funded in the first place.

12   This situation is a bit like the TV game show Jeopardy, where one has to guess the questions. In our case, if one follows back from the starting assumption – without just accepting them – one is led to questions which expose the actual intent. For example, *Yeah, says who?* and *Who gave them a platform and funded their placards?* Of course, a child cannot do this and they have no choice but to accept the assumption that underlies the starting proposition. In this way they come to accept it, as if they had thought of it themselves. And any inconvenient adult would be deplatformed before their crucial tweet hit the numbers.

13   The always need, always claimed by women, for more conversations seems to nicely illustrate one of life's fun paradoxes, in that the real need is for the exact opposite.

I appreciate that saying this demonstrates my need to have a conversation about my desire to deny women a voice. Women have been silenced for long enough, said no man ever.

14   With no regard for need, precedent, practicality or cost: *The government should...(provide free ladies hair care products, liposuction on demand, place*

White men over 50 on a societal danger register, give women a double vote and spa vouchers, etc.).

No items on this list have been made up.

15 For an historical example of this multi-layered, multi-generational approach, which incorporates the whole gamut of motivations from the strongest deliberations to weak, even unwitting, endorsements, let us consider the way that the public attitude with respect to gay rights has been transformed: Here we have a project whose components, which included the print media, the entertainment world, various (hidden) funding benefactors, progressive intellectuals, political activists, malcontents and voluble gays themselves, operated under the apparent ultimate authority of the UN, to dismiss religious objections, ridicule opposition as bigots, fund lobbyists, create positive and sympathetic scripts and characters in TV and movies, support activist groups and alter the law, and all operated in accord with each other, although this was seldom explicitly stated. It was more than just fortuitous that such convergence of effects occurred, but a little less than a full conspiracy; as if (in the ultimate flight of whimsical fancy) all the world's top homosexuals sat around a big table on megalomaniac mastermind Blofeld's island, planning it all out. In actuality, once a momentum with the gay rights project was started, each aspect ran at its own innate speed, drawing sustenance from the other aspects and only occasionally requiring a deliberate, although unseen, guiding hand

Returning to our thesis, with respect to creating future concerns and attitudes, we must imagine *Newsround* playing the same sort of supporting role and having the same sort of end effect in the minds of our children as discussed above.

This effect of changing the public perception of their reality may be regarded as a good thing if it is something that you agree with: for example, if you had a strong personal or principled interest in Gayworld. However, the particular point here is that, as a principle, one should not endorse such influence as you approve of on your children, unless you also wish to accept the same right for others to welcome other opinions, which you do not hold, to be also part of the same opinion forming process.

16   Emma, Lily, Taylor and Ariana. My four little ponies of the apocalypse. It would be wonderful to be able to say: *Thank goodness, children are not being exposed to the dreck pedalled by such fluffy-brained, squeaking fembots.*

Those 12 year old girl media celebrities listed above who know nothing of life but privilege and attention, have been too easily duped into fancying themselves as spokeswomen, for *actual* women, on the very issues they know absolutely nothing about. It is not an accident that they are placed in this position. I refer to them as 12 years old, but know that they are in fact childless women over 30. However, their intellectual age is 12, as their souls are 666.

17   The Viewer Numbers Counter on BBC video podcasts of, taking one typical example, female football, gave lie to the notion that there was a wide female interest in the sport that somehow the patriarchy had been supressing. This held true even for important national games. Of course, females can be interested in football and play it as much as they wish. It's just that most don't, because they don't want to, because they're girls. Of course, males can be interested in Love Island and receive daily updates as they wish. It's just that most don't, because they don't want to, because they're men. I note the number counter was removed as it exposed this truth of the true level of female interest in certain activities.

18   See James Brown and Lucio Pavarotti singing *It's a Man's Man's Mans's World* as a duet. I realise that I have referenced this song elsewhere in this work. Doing so here again is because, now that the song comes from a different cultural age, it is able to shine a light on more natural ways in which men and women can relate to each other. And, as a man, it perfectly sums our relationship to females in one line: *He's nothing, nothing, without a woman or a girl!*

It's only a little song, but songs are magic and can speak great truth to the heart.

Actually, see either of them singing anything.

5: **The Holocaust**

1   We have already considered how emotionally manipulative daily news and certain social justice curricular elements serve as precursors of anxiety in the mind of a child. Not able to properly understand and process distressing information, the child's mind is constantly off balance, always finding itself

short of comprehension before the next info stream arrives. There occurs a snowballing momentum of everything that is not understood and, being wired for empathy, the child is often not able to ignore such. This results in those information streams becoming weaponised. Depression is often a product of excessive anxiety and stress reaching overload. The Holocaust is not just another add-on to this effect, it is a power boost to it.

2   This is not strictly speaking true as there has been much scholarly (and unscholarly) revision. However, this has not escaped, or been allowed to escape, from the figurative concentration camp into which alleged anti-Semites are interned without trial. This is a topic explored at risk, and we will not do so here. You've got be realistic about the circumstances in which you live.

3   This obvious fact, found affirmation from within the Jewish community itself; Israeli cabinet minister, Shulamit Aloni, candidly noted in regard to a question regarding anti-Semitism: *It's a trick we always use when from Europe somebody is criticising Israel, then we bring up the Holocaust. When in this country [USA] people are criticising Israel, then they are anti-Semitic!* For why? – quoting her own words: [to]…*justify everything we do to the Palestinians.* She said it, no Gentile public figure would have dared! Credit where it is due! Candidly conceding this gigantically divisive issue on air is an excellent example of Jewish chutzpah!

The same chutzpah is necessarily continually invoked in maintaining public sympathy as the eternal victim, despite being the wealthiest, most politically well-connected and influential group in most Western nations, and the undoubted controllers of global finance.

4   *It is imperative for us to make less of a display of our pain, to shout less about our losses. It is time we understood that crying and wailing…is mostly evidence of emotional infirmity, of a lack of culture of the soul…. You are not alone in this world, and your sorrow cannot fill the entire universe…when you put on a display only your own grief, only your own pain, it shows…disrespect to others' grief, to others' sufferings.*

Josef. M. Bikerman. *Rossija i russkoe evreisTVo* [Russia and Russian Jewry]. 1924. Quoted from *200 Years Together* by Aleksandr Solzhenitsyn

Bikerman is Jewish and he was referring to the situation in Russia prior to and after the Bolshevik revolution. He was not popular among his fellow Jews for proferring such advice.

5   We recall the time pressure that home and school life is under. Some parents may have the interest and be able to find the time for such discussion within their home schedule, but very few teachers within their class schedules. We note, with sad experience, how all similar quality talk time with pupils quickly segues, under intolerable time constraints, from cursory to travesty to invisible. e.g., learning conversations, termly target consultations and pupil social reviews.

6   Pictures show confusion with WW1, stuka as a fighter plane, Swastika'd Lancaster attacking London in the Blitz, post-war Mk22 Spitfires, etc.,…Grrr!).

7   I am of course referring to our native stock children, some other ethnicities are well acquainted with the concept by their culture; some even by direct experience.

8   There is a double benefit of the focus on the Holocaust as it shines a powerful light of extra interest on the war itself, although at risk, as the author has noted, of dwarfing its parent topic to the extent that many children come to believe that the war was only about the extermination of Jews by Germans. Such a view is not easily countered as default knowledge of the war, typical in my 1960's schooldays and especially among boys, by means of remarks from the then plentiful war service relatives, random wartime memorabilia, boys' comics, Airfix kits, war themed toys and *All Our Yesterdays,* being now distant memories. As a reminder of those not so distant days, my first school still had its bomb shelters.

9   A truly impressive list of historical persecutions, the which, for continued employment's sake, is best accepted at face value.

10 This fact, not that the barrier exists but that a reference is made to it, could – and probably would – be considered and reported as anti-Semitic. We have noted that Holocaust sensitivity has resulted in recent definitions of anti-Semitism to include not just any criticism, but even reference to Jewishness or Israel that is not explicitly supportive. Noting double standards does not help a person so accused.

Suppressing counter-narratives is the flipside of this constant invocation of the Holocaust as a testament to unsurpassed Jewish victimhood. Continuous powerful efforts are made to suppress discussion of, for example, the unsavoury and indisputably leading Jewish role in the Bolshevik Revolution, and especially their murderous excesses which exceeds the magic six. We can easily understand why; such discussion undermines Jewish pretentions to moral authority grounded in their self-designated status as history's preeminent and eternal victims. Likewise, Jews endeavour to maintain precisely the kind of intense group solidarity they decry as immoral in Whites. Ditto for upholding traditional culture and institutions in their own communities.

This is the tunnel we enter into when we establish the Holocaust as a fundamental part of the curriculum.

11 Only Jewish historians and cultural commentators are permitted to discuss this topic, although these also face ruin as 'self-hating Jews' for doing so.

12 From D. Goldhagen's *Hitler's Willing Executioners* which posits a universal German guilt and suggests a racial psychopathy. Denying, or even discussing, the nature of such guilt leads a German swiftly to jail with Gestapo-like efficiency. The irony is colossal, although pointing this out is legally not permitted and does not lessen the sentence.

The other great truth that this study reveals, although not intentionally, is *Vae Victis*; history is written by the winners. And, as always, the difference between a war hero and a war criminal is victory.

13 I am referring to Jewish journalists. There is of course no gene sequence yet discovered that codes for this, however, the argument is more polemical than scientific. It being inferred that there is some, presumably, behavioural influencing genes that predispose us Europeans to irrationally and suddenly choose to pogrom Jews – for no reason whatsoever. This conclusion is, I believe, unlikely and unnecessary; and in any case could be applied to all other peoples among whom the massacre of outgroups is not hard to find. Some ancient and, frankly, weak-willed tribal incidents aside (e.g., The Glencoe Massacre; ~ 30 victims), we in mainland Britain have avoided this tendency- presumably, we must then have kindlier genes. This 'coded in the genes' argument is revealing, as it distracts from examining the facts that have led to incidents of anti-Semitism and instead transfers to the host population the entire blame.

14 In this view, Scotland is presented as a crucial hub in the slave trade, has an inglorious role in British Imperialism, was intolerant of Irish and Highland immigrants and brutally exploited its own people as peasants, workers or soldiers. And it always oppressed women. Such poor treatment of our own

apparently continues in our age with racism, sexism, homophobia, transphobia *et al.*

15   See modern Germany as an example of this force in action. The shame and self-hate of post war Germans is too palpable for comfort. English philosopher, Sir Roger Scruton, has termed this oikophobia, hatred of one's own country and culture, and describes this phenomenon as a particularly Western affliction. This partly explains the ease in finding from among native malcontents those who would destroy all to assuage their own failure on someone' else's account. This other account they would righteously rifle includes our children's well-being. They are the camp kapos of our society and they are well represented in the world of education, particularly amongst the academic levels where curricular content is planned.

16   c.f., My letter to Teaching Scotland. 8th April, 2019 the globalist anti-teacher propaganda rag mag of the GTCS:

HOLOCAUST CPD

I see that there is now a CPD course for the Holocaust, established and funded by an organisation apparently dedicated specifically to this end.

There is no shortage of resources concerning, lessons about, and wider reference to, the Holocaust in our schools. And I would content that there is no need for more, and especially no need to embed it further within our curriculum as the developers of this programme wish. The end result of this development will be more guilt by association for our children and further demonization of the Germans, although the promotors will obviously deny this. Primary school children are particularly vulnerable in this respect, as it is clear to me from experience that, although they can appreciate the facts, they cannot context it or embrace the reality. It is not an appropriate topic at their age. Except as a component of studying the war, the Holocaust is such a politicised and divisive topic, it has no place in our schools.

Embedding the Holocaust in our curriculum is the harbinger of further embedding it in our society which itself, in the great irony that is human intention, leads people to indifference and the anti-Holocaust narrative which daily grows stronger. Eventually the circle is completed when those who refuse the Holocaust guilt or question any aspect of it, find themselves the victims of intolerance, coercion, de-platforming and finally the law and jail time. As we see throughout Europe.

And so the question I posit; is there no escape from the Holocaust for us Gentiles here in Scotland, already has its answer.

(You probably know already, dear reader, that it was not published.)

17   See Finkelstein's *The Holocaust Industry: Reflections on the Exploitation of Jewish Suffering* and *Beyond Chutzpah: On the misuse of anti-Semitism and the abuse of history*. Finkelstein is Jewish. He has suffered the fate of all Hebrew prophets among his own people. We Gentiles generally respect, perhaps too much, intellectual critics of our own history, habits and heroes. We willingly and rationally debate uncomfortable issues of our legacy and can accept uncomfortable conclusions about ourselves; I believe that this tradition, or at least its extent, is unique amongst peoples.

18   This dynamic was recently illustrated by the launching of the new Israeli "Peace Plan." during the 75th Holocaust Anniversary Commemoration. NB. This is referring to this perception, and not commenting on the plan itself whose merits I am unqualified to comment on.

19   The loss of a teaching job (senior teacher in school management) has already happened for questioning the suitability of Holocaust studies, and not for denying the Holocaust or having a secret Nazi past.

20   It may be regretted by the thinking public that teachers are so woefully inadequate to the material, but assuredly this acquiescence has been factored into the decision to introduce this topic; as it is necessary to its intent that when first nailed down in infant Gentile conscience it meets no resistance to impede the further stages of reinforcement of Jewish victimhood and Gentile guilt via TV, media, law and entertainment. On this guilt rests reparations, Israeli ambitions and the wider subversion of our political and cultural life to this end. To this end, indeed, the quasi educated teacher is vastly preferable, they have seen *Schindler's List*, the bulldozer dumping the ragged bodies completes their necessary study. There is thusly no one to prevent the full impact of the message on the childish recipients in class – our children absorbing guilt on industrial scale.

6:   **Multiculturalism**

1   Luckily, I pack my own protection; *Ha, ha!,* can't be sacked if you've already been sacked. Although you can of course be de-platformed and ruined, which will eventually happen following a reading of this sentence.

2   Multicultural advocates argue that no distinction should be made between native stock and ethnic-others in terms of access and benefits. However, when this position does not yield a tribal advantage, the opposite argument, that a distinction should indeed be recognised as a counter to racism, is then adopted. #Whitey Always Racist.

Obviously, the access to school resources and benefits directly connects to wider issues of entitlement; however, I resist the siren call to further explore this rocky shore of privilege politics all the better to avoid early shipwreck.

3   These could include issues regarding curriculum content, religious concessions, gym compliance, diet and lunch arrangements, gender exclusions, etc. It would be professionally dangerous to refer to the potential of gaming the system for benefits, children exploiting the same for convenience, or certain ethnic-other displays of cultural displeasure that feature spitting, biting and hyperbolic threats of violence against classmates and teachers, and so I will not do so. And in wider society in the form of; unmerited preference across various domains, new norms in the selection, admission, hiring and promotion. A parallel legal system silently evolves to enforce different standards of justice – and, of course, token apologies leading eventually to cash reparations.

4   When thinking of this issue, we generally view the school in isolation and therefore struggle to make sense of the evident dysfunction, at best vaguely aware of a hazy complexity of inchoate forces powering it. Properly considered, however, our topic here is a microcosmic focus on a civilisational-scale event, involving a great turning of forces which are hundreds of years in the making; this process of societal change is arguably comparable in scope to Europe's religious reformation or the evolution of modern democracies.

One speculates when studying the ending of empires why their concerned citizens were never able to avert the catastrophe they knowingly faced, and which they knew that their children would inherit; in examining our school system, we shall have a privileged access to an answer.

5   To be fair to multicultural advocates and Leftist activists they never adopted the economic argument. They were about principles. Their championing of the replacement population was for reasons of principle; they do so as an affront and rebuke to the native European population and its culture.

6   This is the tale that cannot be told, except privately.

7   I'm a Shakespeare scholar, I cannae help myself! Everything clever or nicely phrased that I think of, I realise that he's got there before me.

...good things of day begin to droop and drowse, and night's dark creatures to their prey do rouse.

True, the image is stolen, but from the best of sources.

8   It's hard to believe, but I was truly surprised to be told by a well-meaning foreigner that the language spoken in the Garden of Eden, guid Scotch, sounded like snarling dogs. I thanked her for the compliment. Out of a high regard for her tasty, native cuisine with its various toppings, I won't say where she came from.

9   Many of the multicultural benefits do not need to be proselytised as they unequivocally recommend themselves. e.g:

National Guidance for Responding to Female Genital Mutilation in Scotland

School Bomb Plan

A fully funded and full-time diversity team to tackle in-house incidents of racism

School policy for 'Threatening and offensive racist language, gestures or behaviour'

#School-based Sexual Minority Youth of Colour Community Worker

'Slavery Not Tolerated Here' school policy

School Website Pride: *We are proud to say that we listen to the lived experience of marginalised ethnic, alternatively-bodied and gender groups, and make changes to the language we use to make our school more welcoming and supportive.*

Who Wants to be a Millionaire. Question 1:. In multicultural theory is home-grown terrorism and rape gangs part of Diversity, Inclusivity, Equity or all of them? A, B, C, or D?

10   containing Pakistani ~~paedophiles~~ gynaecologists ~~welfare queens~~ wise negresses, Congoid ~~spearchuckers~~ professors, ~~violent~~ brilliant black ~~drug dealer~~ Tesla, ~~psychopathic~~ decent shopkeeping ~~Jihaidists~~ lads, hijabbed ~~grievance~~

~~mongers~~ aeronautical engineers, Somali ~~Uber rapists~~ starship captains, Afghani ~~goat herders~~ geneticists, all making Britain a better place despite persecutions by racists.

There is a school version of this visual warfare that ensures continuous race replacement coverage is brought to the eyeballs of pupils and parents alike. This can readily be seen in all the Scottish school promotional literature, which, like TV adverts in this respect, features surprisingly few, or even no, native White children – e.g., A recent Edinburgh city school info sheet contained a picture of Edinburgh pupils; these being Chinese, mixed race, Black and Asian. As a multicultural advocate tweeted to White parents regarding this observation: *This picture is to get you used to not seeing yourself because you will soon no longer exist. LOL.*

11   I refer to intelligence as the school queen because I do not regard this as the most important factor of school success, far less academic success. I am not entirely sure what the king is, but feel that having a respectful demeanour is a safe bet. With this present, people can work together regardless. If we can have a Sparta-like arrangement with two kings, let's promote conscientiousness.

12   The coward's caveat: *Some of my best friends are..., I wish to apologise in advance for any offence my thoughtless language may have caused..., unfortunately this innocent remark was taken out of context..., Regretfully, I disappointed myself when I ..., however, I no longer hold those beliefs,...* Etc., etc.

13   As pride properly rests on an achievement against odds, one would rightly wonder what there is to be proud about; as opposed to being resigned, accepting, pleased or (honestly) just indifferent.

It's not really pride that is being displayed by school management, but safety-seeking conformity and self-regard for their supposed open-mindedness. The website refers to pride as a subliminal suggestive of how we are to think of this wonderful expression of multicultural wonderfulness. At a deeper level it is meant to evoke the same positive associations with the whole omnibus of multicultural memes – racial justice, equality, inclusion, etc. Even at first contact with multiculturalism, via a school's website, we are faced with bombastic claims and disingenuousness.

14   As already occurs in Sweden. This publicly funded, of course.

15 Sweden again, ever our instructor in future school multicultural dystopia. See my Likabehandlingsplan which explores their journey to Nordic Nivana via self-extinction.

16 TNS, AYTK, BNYB: i.e., He's two naans short (of a rogan josh), Awa yous tae روشمیر, Buenas noches ya bass.

17 I'll be Elvis. No.47 and No.3 are still up for grabs.

18 If properly examined, the infamous claims of racism everywhere in public and social life show nothing of the sort. Even so-called extreme examples, for example, the chants and disparaging remarks directed at Black football players were not, as claimed, evidence of institutional racism in the game, but part of a tradition of such directed at opposing team players. And, minus the colour identification, were no different (or, rather, just as bad) as those directed at White players. In the context, the appellation 'White' added to wee fat cheating c**t, or ginger diving b*****d, was senseless. I have heard a player told to return to his s**** s****** homeland, this being Aberdeen; had this player not been White, this would be recorded as racial abuse and brought down the law, instead of widespread laughter amongst opposing fans. Of course, ethnic-others on your own team were always warmly embraced and generously celebrated; their otherness irrelevant. (e.g., The Justin Fashanu celebratory chant: *He's black, he's gay, he plays for Airdrie!*) This racial reality is never mentioned by MSM. Disgracefully, we still have an organisation dedicated, and publicly funded, to keeping this race bigotry lie alive; having no leader with the moral courage to call it out and demand defunding of these race hustlers.

With respect to primary schools in Scotland, there was no such thing as White racism. And even alleged prime examples are better explained otherwise. Of course, if one wishes to find evidence for such, it is easy to twist any expression or interest to this end, e.g. Racist Rabbie Burns and even Burns' Week itself, which deliberately excludes famous (but unknown, due to racism) POC poets. And continuing the list for fun; flesh-coloured crayons, counting above ten, white (power) socks, milk, the Black Watch, opera, bi-pedal locomotion, etc., etc.

19 Every aspect of which from the training of the counsellors and lawyers to the compensation pay-outs is levied to the public purse.

20 Men are particularly vulnerable in this respect for reasons that relate to prejudice and also, being frequently a singular presence in a school and,

anyway, otherwise isolated by their sex, they make an easy target for maliciously inspired, ruinously intended, secret reporting of bad-thought to school management or other agencies.

21 Jelly Babies are a particular risk in this respect. And imagine if Black Jacks still existed; that would cause some fun down on the plantation!

22 These are the bogus professors who can refer to the need to decolonize the Eurocentric curriculum with no sense of their own absurdity. Perhaps we should start by decolonising their funding. They always have your money, a platform and a receptive audience of variously gendered fembots; just as if they were secretly favoured. I have explored this topic in my Relentless: The Death March to Educational Excellence.

23 Should a Swede have replied (admittedly unlikely) in kind to this remark: *And if you're so proud of where you're from, why don't you go back there!* They would probably have been arrested and, more than likely, lost their job.

24 'Whiteness' – the abstract 'social construct', which must be 'erased' if social progress is to be made. Apparently, it is not directed at the people, but only at their manifestation and physical presence. This is the latest Talmudic sophistry our enemies use to mask genocidal race-hate as progressive social change. Whites can be allowed to continue to exist as long as they abandon any sense of their own identity and their skin colour. But don't try blackface as a solution.

We look forward to the call for the elimination of 'Blackness', 'Muslimness', 'Orientalness' and 'Jewishness'. Not the people, obviously, just the harmful and divisive social constructs, and their physiognomic and dermatologic manifestations.

25 Beat this for mixing references and metaphors. I exceed myself!

26 The loss of being able to say 'our' to a class of children (our history, our ancestors, our music, etc.) is a crucial loss of pupil personal engagement with lessons that connect to culture and history. It is wonderful little word as it establishes the link between you that supersedes the age and status differences. Of course, one could still say it at risk of implying exclusion to others and/or with an uncomfortable self-consciousness.

27 Specifically, the realities of racial psychometrical differences and evolutionary psychology; in this context, our outgroup preference, charitable impulses,

openness, trustworthiness, logical thinking, self-restraint, and reasonableness is our undoing when faced with others who do not generally share these habits as an ethnic package.

28 Ask the Swedes for how quickly this goes. Better do it quickly, unless learning Pashto!

29 By biology we mean kin and ethnicity and, to the extent that such qualities stand extra to race; intelligence, time preference, delinquency, conscientiousness, etc. Without conscious control for such, social foundations will ultimately be inadequate to withstand multiculturalism.

7: The UN

1 You, maybe? And me.

2 Sign o' the times: I have been told that this word has been repurposed and assigned a sexual aspect. I, of course, mean it in the old-fashioned sense; be curious, not bi curious.

3 There are many studies which have exposed the UN as being corrupt, inept, wasteful, ineffective and criminally negligent (and just criminal) to a singular extent. Indeed, without personal study by the concerned citizen to confirm this for themselves, the degree of venality would not be believable. Likewise, the extent to which they can (almost) cover up the plunder of resources and funds.

Of course, most of its staff are just paper-shifting droids, pulling down top dollar for writing garbage, translating it into 500 languages, photocopying this x 10 million, then shredding-and producing a report. However, at its deal-making and project level (the executives, ambassadors and experts) the UN is arguably the most corrupt organisation on the planet. It boils my blood to see it, a bureaucratic bully and parasite, staffed by grifters and fanatics, claim the mantle of moral authority. *Grrr*! [I've just had a cup of tea and calmed down. Apologies for the rant, but...*Grrr*!]

Of course, our concern here is not with its myriad forms of corruption, but with the impact of its ambitions on our schools and our own children therein.

4 This is the term sometimes used to describe the project fronted by the world's most powerful banking, media and political interests, acting in concert to globalise the world economy, champion various sexual and gender projects and

convert Europe from nation states to racially multicultural polities, centrally controlled – *Oh, let me guess* – probably by them. This agenda is usually described as an extension of human rights, justice and equality. It is sometimes disparagingly referred to as the Globohomo Project.

Ideologically, I suppose it would be fair to describe it as a programme designed to facilitate the transmission of the various Cultural Marxist ambitions, and especially those which connect to the transformation of Europe and the European family.

5   A global bank has recently been nakedly showing its globalist hand in a poster campaign extolling the benefits of multiculturalism in Britain, but without mentioning Rotherham *et al*. The current poster (Jan 2020) claims that a liking for square sausage (a Scotch fry-up favourite) is a sufficient patriotic pedigree to be a Scot. No blood, no family, no cultural connection required – and this claim was not made as a joke! One thousand years of history reduced to a beef pattie preference; how's that for buying nationhood cheap! And selling it! Anyway, who gave HSBC the right to confer 'Scot' on anyone it liked? Chutzpah exceeds itself; thusly illustrated the *lèse majesté* of a bank board! These are the funders of our destruction, their contempt for us radiates from their posters. *Grrr!*

We wonder whether a liking for gefilte confers Israeli citizenship on migrants? I'll check with the bank and revert.

6   The Scottish Government recently funded, under UN and EU auspices, an African refugee to mock and deride in a kinetic 'poem' – him reciting a full-blown, anti-White rant while dancing half-naked in the National Portrait Gallery – our various historical Scotch worthies for their racism and whiteness, and his apparent felt exclusion as a result of this. The degree of loathing of us by this ingrate and parasite is truly off the International Freeloader charts; and the degree of self-loathing by the Scotch political class to countenance and facilitate funding of such a project shows something rotten in the state of Scotland. Any native Scot who is thinking of applying for funds to Liberia to return the compliment, let me know how it goes. O – just remembered! – they don't have a national gallery; perhaps mocking their famous cannibal gangs would be the best equivalent.

7   The Scottish Government's recently abandoned 'Named Child' scheme, which would transfer official responsibility for a child's welfare to a named

representative of the state, whether wanted or needed or not, is an example of the extension of the UN mandates to domestic politics that we are here discussing. This initiative failed this time round. This is a warning of the tyrannical and anti-family nature of such forces. And too, a harbinger of what to expect when such justice advocates enjoy power. See following entries.

8   I suppose I must be. Both questions have been sarcastically asked of me.

9   The number of such busybody organisations sticking their noses into other people's family business, while sticking their fingers into the public purse, is astonishing. One cannot help but think: Don't they have their own family to worry about? Although, one knows the answer is no!

It is instructive to consider how easily such groups have platform access in Britain, but not a single significant figure has been allowed a counter voice on the various socially transformative topics such groups champion; and then wonder, why this is.

10   This quote from the California Healthy Youth Act in 2015, but only now are its controversial provisions starting to take effect in classrooms. Under the auspices of health, the law says it will equip students to develop 'healthy attitudes' on 'gender [and] sexual orientation,' among other things. It also says it will inform students about the 'effectiveness and safety of all FDA-approved contraceptive methods,' and facilitate 'objective discussion' about 'parenting, adoption, and abortion.' The nature of the teaching materials and particularly the 'sex health kit' are of particular concern. This project filters all the way down to nursery, for infancy is no protection to exposure to explicit sexual content.

Judicial precedent is cited in claiming that 'parents do not have a constitutional right to excuse their children from portions of the school curriculum that they find objectionable.'

As compensation from excising parental rights with 'may not excuse their children from this instruction', the state (as if generously!) allows parents who disagree with the state's LGBTQ+ position to advise their children at home that they disagree with such lessons. Although such disagreement would have to be judiciously worded to avoid a reporting, accidental or otherwise, of wrong-speak to your child which could end with a visit to your home by state welfare officers and the police with warrants. The police officers are, of course, armed. And, as the resisting parents are tased, comes the thought: Take that, racist transphobe Whitey! This situation has already occurred and is fated to be a commonplace in all Western nations. Concerned parents will be demonised, marginalised and jailed as necessary. Tolerance is not extended to such intolerants!

We have already heard rallying calls that teachers who hold 'intolerant' views, or are sceptical of multicultural benefits, or uncomfortable with promoting the further sexualisation of children's worldview, should be removed from their post. Such has happened, although not yet in Scotland, so far as I am aware. But other countries further along the project curve have actioned this with sackings. Somewhere, someone in a British school will be jailed for hurting someone's feelings by making a transphobic facial expression, or for not liking chapatis. Perhaps Scotland can claim that distinction, we've not had many blasphemy punishments since Jamie the Saxt went to London.

And what next on the sex menu as a focus for tolerance activism? Gender reallocation rights in pre-teens, redefinitions of paedophilia to be more inclusive of alternative cultural practices, polyamorous families, incest as a lifestyle choice? The opponents (that's the future you) of those developments will at first be marginalised, and as the process cranks up, portrayed as violating the civil rights of children and minorities. This situation is truly a portal to a demonic world with very few limits, short of catastrophe.

Here, we can only make passing reference to such a future, but whatever it is, no matter how currently unacceptable it seems, we should now be able to understand the process of conditioning the public to accept the unacceptable. And the necessary activists are already on the move for what comes next; your consent is irrelevant, only the masters' opinions matter here.

11 It is truly remarkable that out of our thousands of cultural commentators, politicians and edgy comedians only the tiniest rebel band have ever offered any sort critical commentary on the developments we are here considering. This shows a mind-lock of great power. That the MSM would attack you, friends publicly disown you and your employers acquiesce in your firing is, of course, a factor. However, these betrayals themselves merely validate further the mystery of this power.

12 Once the White nuclear family has been destroyed there will be no safety net for our children. Nor protection from predators, even when they operate in large gangs known to the police. This we know as a fact.

13 As an example illustrating the end point as both cause and consequence: 'Last February, the [Canadian] Liberals announced they would spend $30 million over the next five years, and after that, more than $10 million every year in perpetuity – or as long as they are in power – to advance the LGBTQ agenda as part of international aid.[Prime Minister]Trudeau is also committed to pushing abortion globally, with the Liberals earmarking a staggering $7.1 billion by 2030 to promote and provide abortion as part of international aid.'

14 With a combined age of 666, some will point out that poptart hardly applies to the African baby-snatchers, Madonna, Charlize, Angelina and the like. I use this term in reference to their teeny minds, which have resisted the blandishments of wisdom. Scrawny, screeching banshees otherwise describes their appearance. And needing the branks, their situation! Seriously, they are the tragic and sad examples of broken womanhood that we hope may serve as a warning to those girls who can see behind their celebrity.

Bono; what sort of grown man calls himself that you might wonder? But actually his real name is *Cui Bono*, although he does do some *Pro Bono* work for the cause. *No runway too small*, as they say! This demon-general and galactic-scale hypocrite always has a platform open for his pronouncements, as well as a runway for his private jet. We can now see why: he has served his dark master well over the years. This may explain his need of shades in God's sunlight.

15 And too, this employment calms their worst fears of their unworthiness, stemming from the superficial and entitled nature of their lives. Secretly understanding this ruinous mismatch and feelings its workings, they have to double down on the denial. Hence the insane moral fanaticism of their advocacy for the approved causes. This is an example of how guilt works its magic: Lesson One.

16 Although I'm rather partial to the thought of Liberian warlord, General Butt Naked, and sexual violence educator and LGBTQ+ poet, Mzz Starry Daze, as special ambassadors working as a team. Perhaps they could take Leonardo's private jet on a UN cultural enrichment tour. I would approve of that, for they would embody an honest visual representation of the UN agenda.

NB. Lest the reader think otherwise, these are real people. Further, it is not my intent to mock them.

17 I was intending illustrating this genocidal hatred, but found myself so enervated by the examples that I felt it best to leave them out. The reader can explore this as they wish. Hatred of course exists everywhere, although in our society it is not, or was not, a common feature of public life, perhaps this is changing as our febrile times work their charms at large. The curious feature of this hatred directed as us ethnic Whites is that it seems to draw down no particular sanction, whereas the opposite…!

18 The details of this historical guilt are not spelt out in primary school; indeed, they are more effectively absorbed by not being so, letting children infer it emotionally, rather than confuse them by fact and argument. These come later in their education and are repeated, directly and by inference, every day on TV in dramas, investigations, current affairs and history documentaries. In the future, aware (or guilty) adults will look back on this indoctrination as their salad days of White guilt.

19 It is a tragedy that girls on the cusp of womanhood, who are misdirected to false and self-damaging activism, should find themselves among hellion-mothers who provide, by their mere presence, the best example of what NOT to do with your life. Such young women are seldom able to shake off the hex and see these living illustrations of barren witchery for what they are. Conversely, the girls could offer an opportunity for redemption to the witches should they even try to rescue some from the same madness that enveloped them when they were young and foolish. Alas, with the Faust-like pact already blood-sworn, few to none of these oblivion-bound hirelings seem to have the wisdom, humility and courage to grasp this opportunity.

20 It has ever been thus in history. Every social revolution comes in under the banner of justice. The fascistic nature and murderous fanaticism of the architects ever stands in direct arithmetical relation to the grandeur of their pronouncements. We should be worried about these world fixers. We have met them before, but not to our advantage.

8: Women Teachers

1 Ever watchful to protect their menfolk from prejudice, feminist activists are of course up in arms about this anti-male sexism and the powerful ladies room networks that silently discriminate against men by institutional handbagism.

In the streets outside of FM Nicola's walk-in wardrobe they can be heard protesting: *No more gynocracy. Men are people too, sometimes!*

2 If there really was a 'patriarchy', this nonsense have been taken care of long ago.

3 We have seen many examples recently of the beliefs that sustain the harmful seven being held well beyond the point even of a direct and cruel meeting with objective reality. So much of the self is invested in embracing these ideas that they cannot be surrendered, even with death. Psychologically, too, women have an even greater difficulty in acknowledging a mistake in their accepting of such ideas, and even more so should the bearer of such bad tidings be a man. As Nicola recently said: *Who do these men think they are? Some of them don't even have hair, except in their ears!*

4 Sisterhood, xxizterhood, ᴣ⚥ᛝterhood, ♫ⴷᛗhood™, etc.

5 Such male teachers are generally kept in a box by female colleagues. And so, they must expect such colleagues to be fired with furious anger against this 'out of their box' behaviour should a male think to challenge the harmful seven orthodoxy; even with a light-hearted quip. The females will understand better than the male who made it, the true intent behind such a remark and act accordingly to nip it, and him, in the bud. He will find that they were not the sisters in arms and 'best mates' he may have hoped for. And maybe she's waiting for you at the end. But, probably not!

Some men accommodate to this hard reality by way of the Stockholm Syndrome; claiming to be, or believing it so, that they are feminists too. Such lack of principle and common-sense brings them no leverage. Women regard male feminists as curs wagging the tail for a doggy biscuit, and rightly sense something dodgy about their motivation.

6 This referencing that this lovely attribute does not scale up so well from nursery to global policy, from sympathy for a little toerag to the same for 40 million. Hence, toxic altruism. This force acts with especial power, as a sort of biological compensation, upon child-bearing age women who have no children. i.e., primary school teachers.

9